BETTER BRIDGE FOR CLUB PLAYERS

Two of the most famous names in British bridge,
Terence Reese and Rixi Markus, winners of
innumerable world and European championships, have
combined to produce a book for players at club level.
It is not a textbook of the usual sort, but a series of
deals that bring out instructive points in declarer's
play, in bidding and in defence. The text is laid out so
that all of the examples are on two facing pages.

This is a rare opportunity for keen players to move
right out of their class.

Also by Terence Reese in the *Master Bridge Series*

DO YOU REALLY WANT TO WIN AT BRIDGE?
  (based on the French text by Pierre Béguin & Jean Besse)
BRIDGE FOR AMBITIOUS PLAYERS

Mini-Masters
MASTER PLAYS IN A SINGLE SUIT
MASTER DECEPTIVE PLAYS

with Roger Trézel
BLOCKING AND UNBLOCKING PLAYS IN BRIDGE
SAFETY PLAYS IN BRIDGE
ELIMINATION PLAYS IN BRIDGE
SNARES AND SWINDLES IN BRIDGE
THOSE EXTRA CHANCES IN BRIDGE
WHEN TO DUCK, WHEN TO WIN IN BRIDGE
MASTER THE ODDS IN BRIDGE
THE ART OF DEFENCE IN BRIDGE
THE MISTAKES YOU MAKE AT BRIDGE

with David Bird
MIRACLES OF CARD PLAY
UNHOLY TRICKS: More Miraculous Card Play
DOUBLED AND VENERABLE: Further Miracles of Card Play
BRIDGE—TRICKS OF THE TRADE

with Julian Pottage
POSITIVE DEFENCE
POSITIVE DECLARER'S PLAY

Better Bridge for Club Players

TERENCE REESE & RIXI MARKUS

LONDON
VICTOR GOLLANCZ LTD
in association with
Peter Crawley
1989

First published in Great Britain 1989
in association with Peter Crawley
by Victor Gollancz Ltd
14 Henrietta Street, London WC2E 8QJ

© Terence Reese & Rixi Markus 1989

British Library Cataloguing in Publication Data
Reese, Terence, 1913–
 Better bridge for club players. – (Master Bridge series).
 1. Contract bridge – Manuals
 I. Title II. Markus, Rixi III. Series
 795.41'5

ISBN 0-575-04526 4

Photoset and printed in Great Britain by WBC Print Ltd, Bristol

Contents

Foreword

Rixi and I have aimed on this occasion to put together a group of deals that club players will find instructive: not squeezes or situations that are simply cute.

Since my approach to the game is generally considered to be fairly academic, while Rixi has a more imaginative style, it might be thought that we would often be in disagreement. But it hasn't turned out that way at all.

We have divided the book into sections on declarer's play, bidding and defence; but these are only rough distinctions, since every example contains points on at least two of these themes.

Terence Reese

PART I—DECLARER'S PLAY

Some of this advice will be familiar, but it is still sound and worth repeating.

After the opening lead don't touch a card from the dummy until you have formed a plan. As declarer, you have an advantage in the early play because you can see two hands in partnership. You can form a plan; this will be difficult or impossible for the defenders until a few tricks have been played.

At the beginning of the play at notrumps the order of thought should be: How many tricks have I on top? Where can I develop extra tricks? What are the dangers?

In a suit contract it is usually simpler to concentrate on losers than on winners.

Don't feel that it is necessary to play quickly when the hand is easy. So far as possible, maintain an even tempo.

When a hand is difficult, don't make this obvious by long trances at each of the early tricks. Maintain your usual rhythm, even if this means that occasionally you might have played a fraction better after a long analysis. The defenders will play better, too, if you attach a label to all the tricky hands.

1. *The Terrible Ten*

How would you set about this hand in four hearts after West had overcalled in spades?

♠ 6 4 3
♥ K 6 5
♦ A K J 8 4
♣ Q 5

♠ A led

♠ J 2
♥ A Q 10 8 7
♦ Q 10 5
♣ A J 4

It was rubber bridge and West began with three top spades. East discarded a low club on the third round and South ruffed. He followed with ace of hearts and a low heart to the king. Is that what you would have done? So would most players. One becomes accustomed to playing certain combinations in a certain way, but it is wise to consider all the circumstances. This was the full deal:

Dealer South   Love all

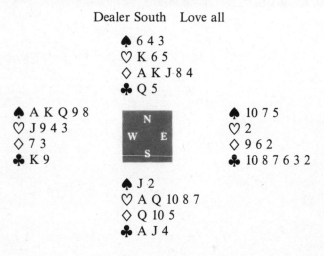

♠ 6 4 3
♥ K 6 5
♦ A K J 8 4
♣ Q 5

♠ A K Q 9 8
♥ J 9 4 3
♦ 7 3
♣ K 9

♠ 10 7 5
♥ 2
♦ 9 6 2
♣ 10 8 7 6 3 2

♠ J 2
♥ A Q 10 8 7
♦ Q 10 5
♣ A J 4

When East showed out on the second round of trumps South's best chance was to take a club finesse. When this lost he was one down.

'I suppose I ought to have made it,' South acknowledged. 'I could have ducked the second round of trumps and let East win if he had the 9 or jack.'

'Isn't it better,' his partner suggested, 'to begin with ace and queen of hearts? You can easily cope with a 4-1 break'. After two round of trumps the position is:

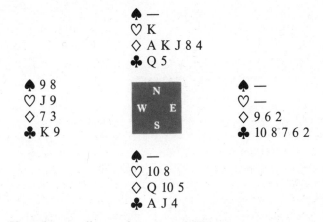

```
                    ♠ —
                    ♡ K
                    ◇ A K J 8 4
                    ♣ Q 5
    ♠ 9 8                             ♠ —
    ♡ J 9              N              ♡ —
    ◇ 7 3          W       E          ◇ 9 6 2
    ♣ K 9              S              ♣ 10 8 7 6 2
                    ♠ —
                    ♡ 10 8
                    ◇ Q 10 5
                    ♣ A J 4
```

'You play on diamonds now and West makes only one trick.'

The declarer thought this over and had to concede that there was some sense in North's remark. 'If I hadn't held the 10 of hearts I would have played it that way', he said.

2. Kings and Commoners

'I've not seen that situation in any of your books', complained the declarer after muddling the play on the deal below. Sorry! But just a little sense is needed. These were the North–South cards:

```
              ♠ 6 3 2
              ♡ 7 4 3
              ◇ 7 5 4 2
              ♣ A 6 5
◇ J led
              ♠ A K 7
              ♡ A K 5
              ◇ A K Q
              ♣ Q 7 4 2
```

South held the sort of hand that only goes to poor players. He opened two clubs and duly rebid 3NT over the two diamond response. West led the jack of diamonds to South's queen.

Needing a ninth trick, South played off ace and king of diamonds in the vague hope of finding a 3–3 break. When this failed, he sought the extra trick by leading a club to the ace and returning a club to the queen. Disappointment, for the full hand was:

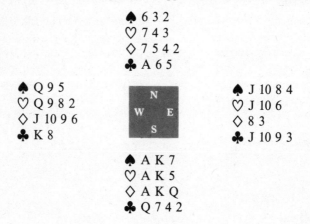

```
              ♠ 6 3 2
              ♡ 7 4 3
              ◇ 7 5 4 2
              ♣ A 6 5

♠ Q 9 5            N            ♠ J 10 8 4
♡ Q 9 8 2      W       E        ♡ J 10 6
◇ J 10 9 6         S            ◇ 8 3
♣ K 8                           ♣ J 10 9 3

              ♠ A K 7
              ♡ A K 5
              ◇ A K Q
              ♣ Q 7 4 2
```

Instead of playing a club to the ace and returning a club to the queen, South should have played low from both hands on the first round of the suit. Then the king appears on the second round.

South was having an unlucky day at rubber bridge, because a few hands later the best play on this deal eluded him:

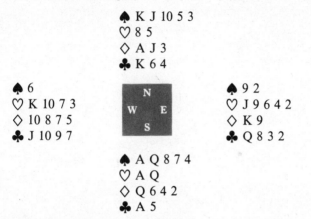

```
                 ♠ K J 10 5 3
                 ♡ 8 5
                 ◇ A J 3
                 ♣ K 6 4
  ♠ 6                          ♠ 9 2
  ♡ K 10 7 3                   ♡ J 9 6 4 2
  ◇ 10 8 7 5                   ◇ K 9
  ♣ J 10 9 7                   ♣ Q 8 3 2
                 ♠ A Q 8 7 4
                 ♡ A Q
                 ◇ Q 6 4 2
                 ♣ A 5
```

Playing in six spades, South won the club lead, drew trumps in two rounds and finessed the jack of diamonds. East returned a heart, the finesse lost, and South was one down. 'I thought the heart finesse was a better chance than finding the diamonds 3–3', he explained.

This was possibly so, but the early play was misconceived. South should play a diamond to the ace and a diamond back. If the queen loses to the king, there will still be time to play for a diamond break; and if the queen holds the trick, again the diamonds can be tested before the hearts. When the diamond king appears on the second round South will not need the heart finesse.

3. *It's Magic!*

After one club by South, one spade by West, what would you bid on the North hand below? If you put this into a bidding competition in one of the magazines you would find half the panel proposing two spades—with what object is beyond all normal understanding. Let us be content with a sensible three clubs.

Dealer South   Love all

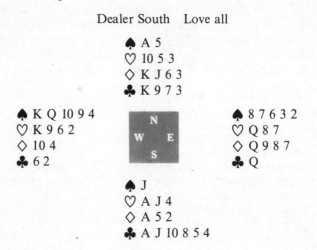

♠ A 5
♡ 10 5 3
◇ K J 6 3
♣ K 9 7 3

♠ K Q 10 9 4
♡ K 9 6 2
◇ 10 4
♣ 6 2

♠ 8 7 6 3 2
♡ Q 8 7
◇ Q 9 8 7
♣ Q

♠ J
♡ A J 4
◇ A 5 2
♣ A J 10 8 5 4

There are ten tricks on top in notrumps, with the clubs breaking 2–1, but you might end in five clubs after this sequence:

South	West	North	East
1♣	1♠	3♣	No
5♣	No	No	No

First, let us consider what would happen in an average game after the lead of the king of spades. South would win in dummy, draw trumps in two rounds, and ruff the second spade. Then, if a knowledgeable performer, he might play king, ace and a third round of diamonds, giving himself the maximum chance for three tricks in diamonds. But no luck! East wins the third round of diamonds and plays a fourth round, which South ruffs. Now he has to tackle the hearts himself and cannot avoid losing two more tricks. It is true that he would have succeeded if he had let West's 10 of diamonds win the second round of the suit, but this might equally have been the wrong play.

There is a very neat solution to this hand. Once both opponents have followed to the first round of trumps, South can be absolutely sure of making five clubs. He draws the outstanding trump and plays the ace and king of diamonds. The North–South hands are then:

♠ 5
♡ 10 5 3
◇ J 6
♣ 9 7

♠ —
♡ A J 4
◇ 5
♣ J 10 8 5

Declarer leads the 5 of spades from dummy—and discards the 5 of diamonds from hand! Say that East takes this trick and leads a low diamond: South simply discards a heart. And if East leads a heart, West will be on play whatever his holding in the red suits. It's magic!

4. *Another Indication*

On many hands you will have to take a decision near the end of the play about the lie of a particular card, usually a queen, sometimes a jack or king. Good players don't often guess wrong, but sometimes they do. More often than not, subsequent analysis will reveal an indication that was overlooked. See how this hand strikes you:

♠ Q 7 4
♡ Q 9 2
◇ A Q 6
♣ K 9 7 4

♠ 6 led

♠ A K 10 9 5
♡ A 7 6
◇ J 10 4
♣ A 6

North–South arrive in the poor contract of six spades. West leads a low trump and South draws three rounds, finding West with J x x while East discards a low heart.

All follow to three rounds of clubs. The diamond finesse wins and on the third round East shows out. South is down to:

♠ —
♡ Q 9 2
◇ —
♣ 7

♠ 10
♡ A 7 6
◇ —
♣ —

When East followed to a fourth round of clubs South thought to himself, 'East has turned up with two spades, two diamonds and four clubs, so he must have begun with five hearts. This makes him favourite to have begun with the king, so I'll discard a heart on this trick and leave him on play.' Unlucky, the full hand was:

```
                 ♠ Q 7 4
                 ♡ Q 9 2
                 ♢ A Q 6
                 ♣ K 9 7 4
  ♠ J 6 3            N          ♠ 8 2
  ♡ K 8                         ♡ J 10 5 4 3
  ♢ K 9 8 5 2    W     E        ♢ 7 3
  ♣ J 8 3           S           ♣ Q 10 5 2
                 ♠ A K 10 9 5
                 ♡ A 7 6
                 ♢ J 10 4
                 ♣ A 6
```

South lost a heart at the finish. He was not in the least abashed. 'I was playing the odds,' he explained. 'I knew the hearts were 5–2, so East was likely to have the king. If East had turned up with only three clubs I was going to ruff and lead a low heart to the 9,' he added.

Let it be said, first, that although East had discarded two hearts by the time of the end-play, this did not affect the mathematical odds. Since he had begun with five hearts the odds were still 5–2 that he held the king.

Mathematically, that is. But there was another consideration— West's lead of a low spade from J x x. Had you forgotten that? Nobody likes to lead from J x x against a slam, perhaps killing partner's Q x. West had chosen this lead only because he had unfavourable holdings in the other suits. If he had held two *small* hearts he would have led a heart, not a trump.

5. *Order of Play*

An understanding of the odds at bridge is not so important as at poker or backgammon, but situations do occur when it is useful to know the chances of an even break in a suit or of a finesse which is not a simple 50–50 proposition. South's mistake on the following deal was a mistake in tactics rather than of calculation.

Dealer North   Game all

♠ J 10 3
♡ A Q
◇ K 6 4 2
♣ A K Q 2

♠ A Q 7 5 2
♡ 9 6 2
◇ Q 8
♣ 10 5 4

♠ 8 4
♡ K J 8 5 4
◇ 9 7 3
♣ J 8 6

♠ K 9 6
♡ 10 7 3
◇ A J 10 5
♣ 9 7 3

Not quite strong enough for 2NT, North began with one club. You may think it natural to respond one diamond on the South hand, but South preferred 1NT on the grounds that this expressed the point count and the balanced distribution. North raised to 3NT and West led a low spade, won by dummy's jack.

Not wanting to give East the chance to obtain the lead, South led the king of diamonds from dummy and followed with a finesse of the jack. West won and led a heart with what the great British player, Maurice Harrison-Gray, used to call a 'cunning look'.

South suddenly found himself off balance. If he finessed the heart and a spade came back he would probably go two down. Should he, perhaps, go up with the ace of hearts and aim to make nine tricks by way of three diamonds, four clubs, one spade and one heart?

Having read somewhere that a 3–3 break of six cards was against the odds, South finessed the queen of hearts. The result was not good for his side.

Initially the chance of a 3–3 break is 36%, so you may think that South was right to take the heart finesse instead of relying on the clubs. But that figure of 36% is based purely on the initial expectation. The bidding—or absence of bidding—by the defenders has a bearing; also the odds change as soon as a few cards have been played. (At the end of a game it may be absolutely certain that six outstanding cards of a suit are divided 3–3.)

The chance of a 3–3 break in clubs was not much less than evens here, and a further consideration was that if West held, say, K x in hearts and four clubs he would be in much trouble when two more diamonds were cashed.

Perhaps you have been waiting for us to say that in one sense this calculation was beside the point? Quite right! South should have tested the clubs *before* taking the diamond finesse.

6. Superstition Confirmed

Suppose you were South, playing in 3NT against a spade lead after West had overcalled with one spade. West leads the queen of spades and you can see:

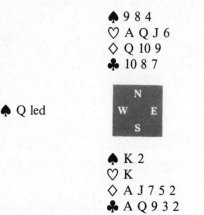

♠ 9 8 4
♡ A Q J 6
◇ Q 10 9
♣ 10 8 7

♠ Q led

♠ K 2
♡ K
◇ A J 7 5 2
♣ A Q 9 3 2

East wins with the ace of spades and returns the suit. How would you play? Would you overtake the king of hearts and take the diamond finesse? That is what the German declarer did in a match between Germany and the Netherlands; without success, for the full hand was:

Dealer West   E–W vulnerable

```
                    ♠ 9 8 4
                    ♡ A Q J 6
                    ◇ Q 10 9
                    ♣ 10 8 7
  ♠ Q J 10 7 5            N          ♠ A 6 3
  ♡ 10 7 5 4 3      W          E     ♡ 9 8 2
  ◇ K 4                   S          ◇ 8 6 3
  ♣ K                                ♣ J 6 5 4
                    ♠ K 2
                    ♡ K
                    ◇ A J 7 5 2
                    ♣ A Q 9 3 2
```

This was the bidding at the other table:

South	West	North	East
—	No	No	No
1◇	1♠	Dble	No
2♣	No	2♠	No
3NT	No	No	No

North's double was negative and his two spades apparently
requested a guard in spades. As he was far from minimum, South
jumped to game.

When West led the queen of spades, East ducked. (This was
good play in general, because in some circumstances it would
make West's discarding easier.) South won and at trick two made
the fine 'extra chance' play of laying down the ace of clubs. When
the king of clubs made its customary appearance ('the king of
clubs is always single') it wasn't difficult for the declarer to
overtake the king of hearts and run the 10 of clubs. When this held,
he cashed the queen and jack of hearts and ended with ten tricks.

Now suppose that West had held K J of clubs and not the king
of diamonds. What a brilliancy then to drop the king of clubs
under the ace!

7. At a Cost

Certain forms of play are deceptive, in the sense that they are frequently overlooked. You may like to test yourself. Suppose that you finish in four spades as South on the deal below. There has been no opposition bidding and West leads the king of hearts.

♠ 10 9 4 2
♡ A 8
♢ K J 9
♣ Q 6 5 2

♡ K led

♠ Q J 7 6 5 3
♡ J 4
♢ Q 2
♣ A K J

There would be no problem if they had led some other suit, but life is not like that. In a pairs event more than half the field won with the ace of hearts, crossed to hand with a club, and led the queen of spades. They hoped that West, with ♠ K x or A x, might be so foolish as to play the honour.

Well, that wasn't likely, especially with K x, and in fact West had a singleton king. A more sensible line would have succeeded, for the full hand was:

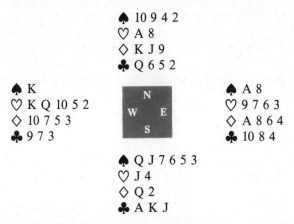

♠ 10 9 4 2
♡ A 8
◇ K J 9
♣ Q 6 5 2

♠ K
♡ K Q 10 5 2
◇ 10 7 5 3
♣ 9 7 3

♠ A 8
♡ 9 7 6 3
◇ A 8 6 4
♣ 10 8 4

♠ Q J 7 6 5 3
♡ J 4
◇ Q 2
♣ A K J

South should play ace, king and jack of clubs, overtaking with the queen. Then he plays the thirteenth club, discarding a heart. Either opponent can ruff—but at a cost.

The same idea appears on this next hand in a rather more difficult form.

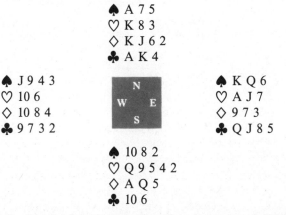

♠ A 7 5
♡ K 8 3
◇ K J 6 2
♣ A K 4

♠ J 9 4 3
♡ 10 6
◇ 10 8 4
♣ 9 7 3 2

♠ K Q 6
♡ A J 7
◇ 9 7 3
♣ Q J 8 5

♠ 10 8 2
♡ Q 9 5 4 2
◇ A Q 5
♣ 10 6

South plays in four hearts after East has opened 1NT. West leads a spade to the queen and East leads back the king. The declarer sees that if he plays on trumps he will lose four tricks unless East has a doubleton ace. A better chance is to play four rounds of diamonds, discarding a spade. Whether West or East ruffs this trick, South can hold the losers to one spade and two hearts.

[23]

8. *There Was a Reason*

Imagine that you are playing in four spades with these cards:

♠ A 5
♥ K 7 3
♦ A Q 5
♣ K J 9 5 3

♣ A led

```
      N
  W       E
      S
```

♠ J 9 7 6 4 2
♥ A 6
♦ K 10 8 2
♣ 7

The bidding has been:

South	West	North	East
—	—	1♣	No
1♠	No	2NT	No
4♠	No	No	No

West leads the ace of clubs and follows with the 9 of hearts, which you win with the ace. You play a spade to dummy's ace, on which East drops the king. How do you assess the situation now?

Most players in a pairs event thought to themselves: 'I can't do it if the spades are 4–1, because I have already lost a club and if West began with ♠ Q 10 8 3 he will make three more tricks. Well, there may be a faint chance of end-playing him, but meanwhile I don't want to go down in a simple contract if East began with K Q of spades alone. So I'll lead a second round of trumps.'

This did not prove a success because the full hand was:

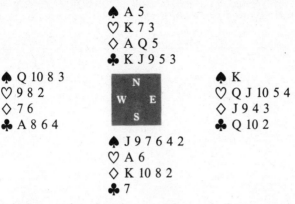

                    ♠ A 5
                    ♡ K 7 3
                    ◇ A Q 5
                    ♣ K J 9 5 3

♠ Q 10 8 3   ♠ K
♡ 9 8 2   ♡ Q J 10 5 4
◇ 7 6   ◇ J 9 4 3
♣ A 8 6 4   ♣ Q 10 2

                    ♠ J 9 7 6 4 2
                    ♡ A 6
                    ◇ K 10 8 2
                    ♣ 7

The declarers who played a second round of trumps missed a significant point: why had West begun with the ace of clubs in front of the suit bid by North? When the king of spades fell from East on the first round of trumps it wasn't difficult to find a reason for the opening lead: West expected to make some trump tricks and wasn't going to risk the discarding of a club singleton.

The clever players took note of this inference and set about a trump reduction. This involved ruffing at least twice in hand. After the ace of spades South played king and another club, then three rounds of hearts, ruffing the third round. The position was now:

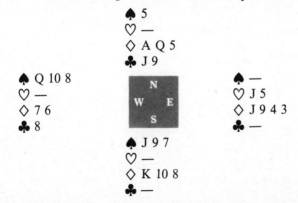

                    ♠ 5
                    ♡ —
                    ◇ A Q 5
                    ♣ J 9

♠ Q 10 8   ♠ —
♡ —   ♡ J 5
◇ 7 6   ◇ J 9 4 3
♣ 8   ♣ —

                    ♠ J 9 7
                    ♡ —
                    ◇ K 10 8
                    ♣ —

From the fall of the cards it certainly looked as though West held two diamonds and one club, so the declarer played two rounds of diamonds, ruffed a club, and followed with a diamond at trick eleven, leaving West on play.

9. A Knowledgeable Air

It doesn't look difficult to land four spades on the deal below. There are nine tricks on top (counting two in clubs) and several chances for a tenth. And South assured his partner afterwards that he knew all about elimination play.

Dealer South   Game all

```
              ♠ Q J 9 3
              ♡ 6 5 3
              ◇ J 6 2
              ♣ Q J 3
♠ 8 4                        ♠ 6
♡ K 10 7 2                   ♡ J 9 8
◇ A K 9 5                    ◇ 10 8 7 4 3
♣ 10 9 6                     ♣ K 8 7 4
              ♠ A K 10 7 5 2
              ♡ A Q 4
              ◇ Q
              ♣ A 5 2
```

The bidding did not take long:

South	West	North	East
1♠	No	2♠	No
4♠	No	No	No

West began with the ace of diamonds. When his partner played the 3 and South the queen, a diamond continuation seemed unattractive, so he tried the 10 of clubs. Dummy's jack was covered by the king and ace. South played a spade to dummy, ruffed a low diamond, and returned to dummy with a second round of trumps. Then he cashed the queen of clubs, led the jack of diamonds from dummy, and with a knowledgeable air discarded a heart from hand.

West won this trick and led a third club to his partner's king. Now East advanced the jack of hearts and the defenders made two heart tricks to defeat the contract.

'I was hoping to find West with just a doubleton club,' South informed his partner. 'Then he has to give me a ruff-and-discard or open up the hearts.'

'Does it make any difference,' North inquired mildly, 'if you let them win their club trick earlier on?'

It does, indeed. When West leads the 10 of clubs at trick two South can let this card hold the trick. Suppose that West then switches to a trump. South ruffs a low diamond, draws a second trump, and leads the queen of clubs from dummy. If East declines to cover, South plays another club to the ace, then enters dummy with a third round of trumps. The position is now:

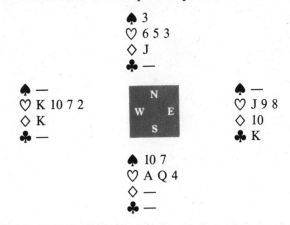

```
              ♠ 3
              ♡ 6 5 3
              ◇ J
              ♣ —
♠ —                              ♠ —
♡ K 10 7 2        N             ♡ J 9 8
◇ K           W       E         ◇ 10
♣ —               S             ♣ K
              ♠ 10 7
              ♡ A Q 4
              ◇ —
              ♣ —
```

Declarer leads the jack of diamonds from dummy and discards his losing heart, leaving West on play. The textbooks call it a loser-on-loser elimination.

10. *Unexpected Winner*

Six spades looks easy on the North–South cards below, does it not? If you treat the South hand as master you can ruff two hearts, discard a club from dummy on the king of hearts, and ruff a club, so losing just one club trick. Looking at it from the other side, you can ruff three diamonds in the South hand and again discard a club on the king of hearts.

Oddly enough, neither of these plans will work when the trumps are 3–0 and the hearts 7–1. You will need to find another solution.

Dealer North   Love all

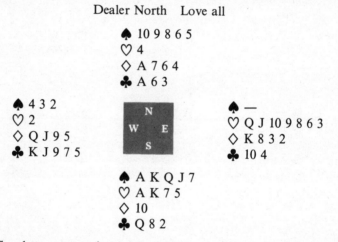

♠ 10 9 8 6 5
♡ 4
◇ A 7 6 4
♣ A 6 3

♠ 4 3 2
♡ 2
◇ Q J 9 5
♣ K J 9 7 5

♠ —
♡ Q J 10 9 8 6 3
◇ K 8 3 2
♣ 10 4

♠ A K Q J 7
♡ A K 7 5
◇ 10
♣ Q 8 2

The slam contract is easy to reach even after an opposing pre-empt.

South	West	North	East
—	—	No	3♡
4♠	No	6♠	No
No	No		

West leads a heart, which runs to the 8 and ace. Noting that the contract will be lay-down if the trumps are 2–1, South cashes the ace of spades. When East shows out, the declarer realizes that he will have to work for the slam. The difficulty is that he cannot cash the second heart early on, because West, no doubt, has led a singleton.

One possibility is to play East for the king of clubs. It seems reasonable to test the diamonds first: diamond to the ace and diamond ruff, spade overtaken, diamond ruff, heart ruff, diamond ruff, by which time East's king has appeared. It is certain now that the king of clubs will lie with West. The position in fact is as follows:

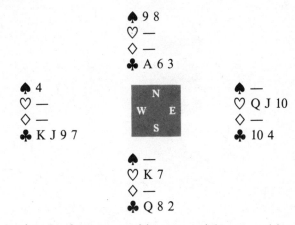

```
                    ♠ 9 8
                    ♡ —
                    ♢ —
                    ♣ A 6 3
   ♠ 4                               ♠ —
   ♡ —          ┌─────────┐         ♡ Q J 10
   ♢ —          │    N    │         ♢ —
   ♣ K J 9 7    │ W     E │         ♣ 10 4
                │    S    │
                └─────────┘
                    ♠ —
                    ♡ K 7
                    ♢ —
                    ♣ Q 8 2
```

Against moderate opposition you might succeed by ruffing a heart, drawing the last trump, and running a club to the 8 and 9. East can—and should—spoil this plan by inserting the 10 of clubs.

So you look for a different plan. Lead the king of hearts, which West must ruff. Now don't overruff. Just discard a club from dummy and West will be left on play.

It's rather odd, if you look again at the original diagram, that West's only trick should be one of his low trumps!

11. *Knavish Tricks*

The deal below was played by the French star, Dominique Pilon, in the 1987 Cino Del Duca Pairs Championship. A strange thing about it is that West took two tricks against South's contract of 3NT—one with the jack of spades and the other with the jack of diamonds.

Dealer East   Game all

In some parts of the world, and especially in America, players commonly open very weak three-bids. The French are not so foolish as to offer hostages to fortune in this fashion. Here East opened a sound three spades and the bidding was brief:

South	West	North	East
—	—	—	3♠
3NT	No	No	No

If you put the South hand into a bidding competition, asking what he should do over an opening three spades, you would find some support for Double, on the grounds that this might enable North to respond 3NT with a spade holding such as Q x. But it's a long shot and on this occasion would not have made much difference.

West led the jack of spades against 3NT and Pilon, the declarer, wisely allowed this to hold, thus effectively killing East's long spade suit. West had to find a switch of some kind and he chose the 10 of hearts. South won with the jack and tested the clubs by laying down the ace. The news was not good, East discarding a spade.

At this point the declarer needed three diamond tricks, or possibly two diamond tricks followed by an end-play in clubs. He ran the queen of diamonds, which lost to the king. East cashed the ace of spades and exited with a spade, leaving:

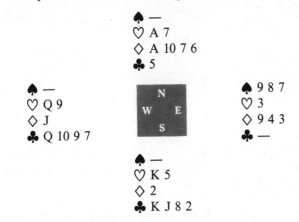

Still needing two extra tricks from somewhere, South led a diamond, on which West's jack appeared. Pilon could have cashed the A 10 and followed with two hearts and a low club, end-playing West, but he found a prettier solution: he allowed West's jack of diamonds to win and claimed the rest of the tricks. East had made the king of diamonds and the ace of spades, West his two jacks.

12. *Early Decision*

When the same contract is played at both tables of a match, sometimes a very slight difference in the play will lead to a different result at the two tables. Take this hand, where both teams arrived at the obvious contract of six hearts:

♠ K Q 9
♡ K J 4 2
♢ A 7 5
♣ K 6 4

◇ Q led

♠ 10 7
♡ A Q 10 8 3
♢ K 8 4
♣ A Q J

You win the diamond lead with the king and note that you will need to develop an extra trick in spades to dispose of the diamond loser. Two questions arise: do you draw trumps before leading a round of spades? Exactly how will you play the spades?

You may think there is no reason why you shouldn't draw trumps immediately. It's not likely, but the diamonds might possibly be 6–1 and you would look foolish if a spade from hand lost to the ace and a diamond ruff followed. But that's a very small chance indeed, and there is another consideration. This was the full hand:

```
                    ♠ K Q 9
                    ♡ K J 4 2
                    ◇ A 7 5
                    ♣ K 6 4
  ♠ A 3 2                              ♠ J 8 6 5 4
  ♡ 7 6 5              N               ♡ 9
  ◇ Q J 10 6 2     W       E           ◇ 9 3
  ♣ 10 8              S                ♣ 9 7 5 3 2
                    ♠ 10 7
                    ♡ A Q 10 8 3
                    ◇ K 8 4
                    ♣ A Q J
```

At one table South played the slam in orthodox, not to say ordinary, fashion. He won the diamond lead and drew trumps, East discarding the 4 of spades and the 2 of clubs. The 10 of spades was won by the king in dummy. South came back to hand with a club and led the 7 of spades, on which West cleverly played low. He could judge that his partner held an odd number. South finessed the 9, losing to the jack. East led a third round of spades and South in due course lost a diamond, to go one down.

'It's a pity I held the 10 of spades', South remarked. 'Otherwise there's no guess, I have to play West for the ace.'

South did not realize that he had made two small but significant errors. Compare the play at the other table. There South won the diamond lead and at once led the 7 of spades from hand. This was good play for two reasons: West (if he held the ace) would have to make a decision before he knew anything about the spade distribution; and the 7 of spades was a better card than the 10, because the play of the 10 would make it clear to West that declarer might have a guess later on.

As it happened, West was good enough—or lucky enough—to take a right view and duck the spade lead. The declarer then drew trumps before leading the 10 of spades. West looked at this for a moment—but a moment was too long. Rather feebly he played the ace and so surrendered the contract.

13. *Better Sight Without Glasses*

Spectators who can see all four hands on a Vu-Graph screen are usually one ahead of players at the table who can see only 26 cards. But sometimes it's the other way round: the player at the table sees something that has escaped the audience, and perhaps the commentators as well.

Dealer North   Game all

                ♠ A K 10 9 7 3
                ♡ 10 6 5
                ◇ A K 10
                ♣ 3

♠ J 8 6 2   ♠ 4
♡ 9   ♡ J 7 4 2
◇ J 9 8 7   ◇ 6 4 3
♣ A 9 6 4   ♣ Q J 10 8 7

                ♠ Q 5
                ♡ A K Q 8 3
                ◇ Q 5 2
                ♣ K 5 2

Playing for a team that was touring South Africa, the Canadian star, Sammy Kehela, became declarer in the best contract, 6NT. The bidding might have gone like this:

South	North
—	1♠
2♡	3◇
3♠	4♠
4NT	5♠ (1)
6NT	No

(1) Promising two aces and a critical king.

West found the safest lead on his hand, the 9 of diamonds. South won in dummy and cashed two hearts, unblocking the 10 when West discarded a club on the second round. Then he crossed to dummy, finessed the 8 of hearts and picked up two more tricks in the suit, while West discarded another club and two diamonds.

The surprise came on the fifth round of hearts, when instead of keeping five spades in dummy Kehela discarded two of them. There was a gasp from the audience, who had expected him to keep five spades and lose a spade and a club at the finish. But Sammy knew what he was doing. After the third diamond had been cashed the position was:

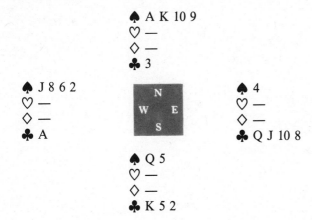

```
                      ♠ A K 10 9
                      ♡ —
                      ◇ —
                      ♣ 3
  ♠ J 8 6 2                               ♠ 4
  ♡ —              ┌──────────┐           ♡ —
  ◇ —              │    N     │           ◇ —
  ♣ A              │  W   E   │           ♣ Q J 10 8
                   │    S     │
                   └──────────┘
                      ♠ Q 5
                      ♡ —
                      ◇ —
                      ♣ K 5 2
```

There had been nothing to indicate the spade break, so the declarer played queen and ace, East discarding. It would have been possible now to cash the spade king and play East for the ace of clubs, but good players can usually read the position at this stage of the play. At any rate, Kehela exited with the club from dummy and made the last two tricks when West had to lead a spade into the K 10.

14. *First Appearance*

The Swedish Open team had almost a runaway win in the 1987
European Championship at Brighton. The Ladies team did less
well, but it included five players who were making their
championship debut. One of these, Lena Kaerrstrand, had a
baptism of fire in the Ladies Pairs Championship, which preceded
the team event. This was her very first board:

Dealer South   E–W vulnerable

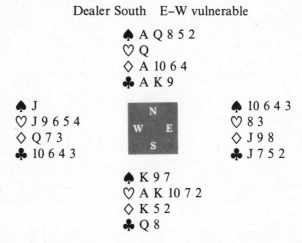

```
              ♠ A Q 8 5 2
              ♡ Q
              ◇ A 10 6 4
              ♣ A K 9
♠ J                                  ♠ 10 6 4 3
♡ J 9 6 5 4                          ♡ 8 3
◇ Q 7 3                              ◇ J 9 8
♣ 10 6 4 3                           ♣ J 7 5 2
              ♠ K 9 7
              ♡ A K 10 7 2
              ◇ K 5 2
              ♣ Q 8
```

Kaerrstrand became the declarer in the excellent contract of
7NT, which in principle depends on one of the major suits
producing five tricks.

West began with a low club, which ran to the jack and queen.
South led the 9 of spades to the ace, on which West's jack
appeared. It would be unsafe (at this point) to return a low spade
to the 7, because West might have played the jack from J 10 alone
or from J 10 x.

To find out more about the hand, South cashed the queen of
hearts, crossed to the king of diamonds, and played off ace and
king of hearts, East discarding a club on the second round, while
two diamonds were thrown from dummy. After two more rounds
of clubs the position was:

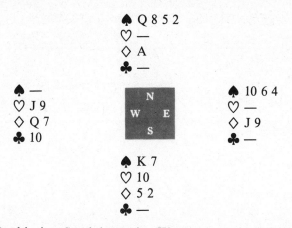

                    ♠ Q 8 5 2
                    ♡ —
                    ◇ A
                    ♣ —

    ♠ —   ♠ 10 6 4
    ♡ J 9   N   ♡ —
    ◇ Q 7   W   E   ◇ J 9
    ♣ 10   S   ♣ —

                    ♠ K 7
                    ♡ 10
                    ◇ 5 2
                    ♣ —

By this time South knew that West had started with five hearts and probably four clubs. She certainly held the queen of diamonds, because if East had held Q J x x she would have inserted an honour when the suit was led from dummy. Thus it looked as though West had begun with jack of spades alone, or possibly a doubleton J 10. At any rate, Kaerrstrand finessed the 7 of spades in the diagram position and so made the grand slam.

Whether any British pair bid—and made—the grand slam in notrumps, we cannot say. In modern Acol the bidding might go:

South	North
1♡	1♠ (1)
2♠	3◇
3♡	4♣
4◇	4NT
5♡ (2)	6♣ (3)
7NT (4)	

(1) Most players, in these days, force only when they have either a strong suit of their own or strong support for partner's suit.

(2) In five-ace Blackwood this would show (depending on the variation) either two aces or one ace and at least one critical king.

(3) North asks for a little extra . . .

(4) . . . which South, who has two important kings and extra values, is able to supply.

15. *Guessing Game*

There are many situations where a declarer seems to have a guess, but one guess is decidedly better than another. For example:

10 5 4

Q led

K 7 2

At some stage in the play East leads the queen of this suit through the declarer's king. South ducks the first round and East then leads a low card of the same suit. Supposing that there is no other indication, do you think that it is an open guess for the declarer to play East for A Q x or Q J x?

You could be wrong, of course, but in general you should play East for A Q rather than Q J. The reason, in simple terms, is that with Q J x East might have begun with the jack, whereas with A Q x he would have had no choice. So you should play him for A Q x.

This is another very common situation of the same kind:

A 10 5

J led

K 9 4

Towards the end of the play West is obliged to open this suit and he advances the jack. This might be from J x x and it might be from Q J x. In general, you should assume that the honours are divided, because with Q J x West might have begun with the queen. It is what is known as the Principle of Restricted Choice: you assume that the defender did not have a choice rather than that he exercised a choice in a particular way.

The declarer on this deal from a ladies international no doubt knew about the principle but perhaps did not recognize its application.

Dealer South   Game all

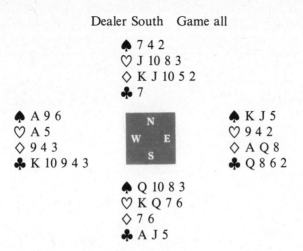

♠ 7 4 2
♡ J 10 8 3
◇ K J 10 5 2
♣ 7

♠ A 9 6
♡ A 5
◇ 9 4 3
♣ K 10 9 4 3

♠ K J 5
♡ 9 4 2
◇ A Q 8
♣ Q 8 6 2

♠ Q 10 8 3
♡ K Q 7 6
◇ 7 6
♣ A J 5

North–South managed to obtain the contract at an economic level when the bidding went:

South	West	North	East
1♣	No	1◇	No
1♡	No	2♡	No
No	No		

Expecting the declarer to be ruffing clubs in dummy, West began with ace and another heart. Deciding now to play for diamond tricks rather than club ruffs, South drew a third round of trumps, then led a diamond to the jack and queen.

At this point Nicola Smith (Nicola Gardener at the time) played the king of spades and followed with the 5. South had to decide whether to play the queen or the 10, and she guessed wrong. Playing the queen led to one down.

This was a restricted choice situation, since with A K 5 East would have had alternative lines of play. She might have led the ace followed by the 5, or she might have begun with the 5. To find her with K J 5 was a better proposition.

Note, also, that East played well. If she had begun with the low card, then South would surely have finessed the 10.

16. *No Need to Panic*

Some of the most interesting manoeuvres in the game involve what may be thought of as a 'second trump suit': that is, using an established suit to force out an opponent's long trumps and so regain control. An instructive example occurred during the 1985 B.B.L. Ladies Trials.

Dealer South   Love all

♠ 7
♡ K 8 7 2
◇ A K 8 5 4 3
♣ A Q

♠ A K 4 3
♡ 4
◇ Q 10 7
♣ K 9 7 6 5

♠ Q J 10 9 5
♡ J 10 9 6
◇ 9 6
♣ J 10

♠ 8 6 2
♡ A Q 5 3
◇ J 2
♣ 8 4 3 2

The North–South cards are not so easy to manage after West has opened one club. North may make an intermediate jump overcall of two diamonds, but it is not certain that South will respond to this. At one table the bidding went:

South	West	North	East
No	1♣	Dble (1)	1♠
2♡	2♠	4♡	No
No	No		

(1) Most British players would hesitate to double with no support for one of the majors, but Italian players, especially, have never had any qualms about this. Their principle is that when you have the values for an opening bid you double.

West led the ace of spades, her partner signalled with the queen, and West played a second round, ruffed in dummy. The declarer played king and ace of hearts, discovering the bad news, and then set about the diamonds, ruffing the third round. The position was then:

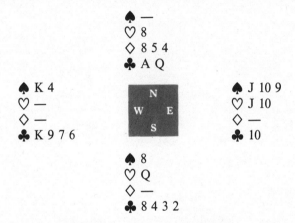

East held the long trump, but South had lost only one trick and the hand was under control. She led a club to the queen and played a winning diamond, forcing East to ruff while South discarded her spade loser. When East returned a spade the declarer ruffed in dummy and led another winning diamond. East ruffed and was overruffed. Then a club was led to the ace and South ended with eleven tricks.

The play does not look difficult, but one declarer made only ten tricks in this contract and one managed to go down.

17. *Second Thoughts Were Better*

As a rule, a declarer taking a finesse hopes it will win. Sometimes he may hope it will lose. This hand was a little special because the result would be equally satisfactory whether the finesse won or lost.

Dealer South   E–W vulnerable

♠ K 7 6 2
♡ K 10 8 3
◇ K 9
♣ Q 9 8

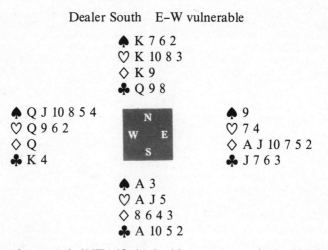

♠ Q J 10 8 5 4   ♠ 9
♡ Q 9 6 2   ♡ 7 4
◇ Q   ◇ A J 10 7 5 2
♣ K 4   ♣ J 7 6 3

♠ A 3
♡ A J 5
◇ 8 6 4 3
♣ A 10 5 2

South opened 1NT, 12–14 in his system, and the bidding continued:

South	West	North	East
1NT	No (1)	2♣ (2)	No
2◇	No	2NT	No
3NT	No	No	No

(1) Since he will be on lead against a notrump contract, West is right not to risk a rather dangerous overcall.

(2) Players always apply the old Stayman on these hands and will doubtless continue to do so. Nevertheless, with honours in every suit there is much to be said for a direct raise in notrumps. Defenders often lead a major suit when there has been no Stayman inquiry.

West's lead of the queen of spades ran to the ace. South played the ace of hearts and followed with the jack, which was covered by the queen and king. Then he ran the 8 of clubs, taken by the king. West pressed on with a spade to dummy's king, East discarding a diamond. South played queen of clubs, then finessed the 10 and cashed the ace. He had made seven tricks and these cards were left:

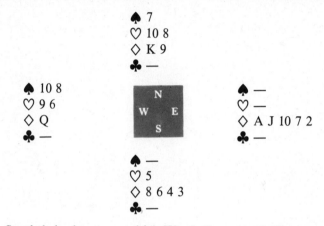

```
              ♠ 7
              ♡ 10 8
              ◇ K 9
              ♣ —
♠ 10 8                        ♠ —
♡ 9 6          N              ♡ —
◇ Q          W   E            ◇ A J 10 7 2
♣ —            S              ♣ —
              ♠ —
              ♡ 5
              ◇ 8 6 4 3
              ♣ —
```

South led a heart, on which West's 6 appeared. The question now was whether to play for the drop or to finesse the 8. The declarer's first thought was that eight of West's black cards were known—six spades and two clubs; why, therefore, play him for longer hearts than his partner, who was marked with just one spade and four clubs? Fortunately for his side, South considered the matter from another angle. East was surely marked with the ace of diamonds, since otherwise West would have overcalled. And if East held the 9 of hearts it would still be safe to finesse, because East would have to return a diamond, presenting the dummy with two more tricks.

18. *Second Lesson*

One of the first lessons a player is taught is the hold-up in notrumps when he has something like A x x in the suit led. As a matter of fact, it is almost as often right to win the second round, sometimes to avoid a switch and sometimes to retain a card of exit. This deal is a trifle artificial, but instructive.

Dealer South   E–W vulnerable

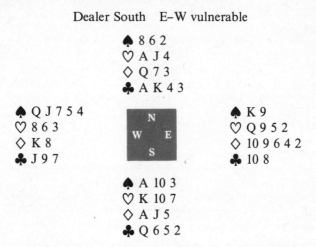

```
                    ♠ 8 6 2
                    ♡ A J 4
                    ◇ Q 7 3
                    ♣ A K 4 3
    ♠ Q J 7 5 4                      ♠ K 9
    ♡ 8 6 3              N           ♡ Q 9 5 2
    ◇ K 8          W         E       ◇ 10 9 6 4 2
    ♣ J 9 7             S           ♣ 10 8
                    ♠ A 10 3
                    ♡ K 10 7
                    ◇ A J 5
                    ♣ Q 6 5 2
```

The bidding is an unexciting 1NT–3NT and West begins with a low spade to the king. This is allowed to hold and East leads a second round. Now most players would hold up again, but this will not ensure the contract.

You can afford to lose four spade tricks, and a better line is to keep a card of exit and hope to force West to present you with a ninth trick in hearts or diamonds. You still need to think about the entries. After winning the second spade cash three clubs, being careful to retain the 2. The position will then be:

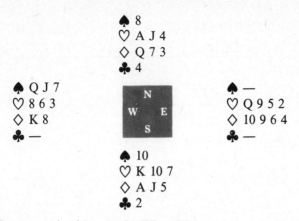

♠ 8
♥ A J 4
♦ Q 7 3
♣ 4

♠ Q J 7   ♠ —
♥ 8 6 3   ♥ Q 9 5 2
♦ K 8   ♦ 10 9 6 4
♣ —   ♣ —

♠ 10
♥ K 10 7
♦ A J 5
♣ 2

Now you exit with a spade. When West cashes two more spades you discard two diamonds from dummy, one heart and one diamond from hand. Now West may lead a heart into your K 10. You cash these and are glad you have kept the 2 of clubs to provide an entry to dummy.

This is another test where the same kind of play is indicated:

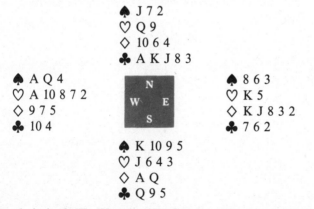

♠ J 7 2
♥ Q 9
♦ 10 6 4
♣ A K J 8 3

♠ A Q 4   ♠ 8 6 3
♥ A 10 8 7 2   ♥ K 5
♦ 9 7 5   ♦ K J 8 3 2
♣ 10 4   ♣ 7 6 2

♠ K 10 9 5
♥ J 6 4 3
♦ A Q
♣ Q 9 5

South is in 2NT. West leads a heart to the king, a heart is returned and West clears the suit. Now South has seven tricks in sight and the best play for an eighth is to cash *two* clubs, then exit in hearts. As the cards lie, West has to lead a spade or a diamond after cashing his heart winners. If West had held a third club South would have had to decide later whether to play for his eighth trick in spades or diamonds.

19. *A Fair Assumption*

The deal below is an example of a form of reasoning which is not in the least difficult but is somehow overlooked by the great majority of players. See how it strikes you.

Dealer East   Game all

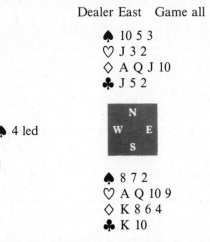

♠ 10 5 3
♡ J 3 2
♢ A Q J 10
♣ J 5 2

♠ 4 led

♠ 8 7 2
♡ A Q 10 9
♢ K 8 6 4
♣ K 10

Not a weak notrump merchant when vulnerable, South opens one heart in second position. It is a question of style whether North should respond 1NT, two hearts, or two diamonds. Let us say that he responds two diamonds and South raises to three diamonds. Now North bids three hearts. This is not forcing in Acol and South passes hastily. So South plays in three hearts after this sequence:

South	West	North	East
—	—	—	No
1♡	No	2♢	No
3♢	No	3♡	No
No	No		

West leads a low spade and East, after a moment's reflection, plays the queen. When this holds he returns a low spade to his partner's jack and wins the third round with the ace. In other words, he started with ♠ A Q x. Now he advances the 8 of clubs. As South, are you going to play him for the ace or the queen, and why?

One point you should be thinking about is that in a pairs event some players, perhaps the majority, will have opened with a weak notrump on your hand. They will play there and probably make it, so you must concentrate on making three hearts—probably your only chance of a good board.

You must assume, therefore, that the king of hearts is well placed for you. What follows from that?

East has already turned up with A Q x in spades. You are placing him with the king of hearts because you hope to make nine tricks in hearts while some declarers may be making only eight in notrumps. If East holds ♠ A Q and ♡ K, can he hold the ace of clubs as well? Surely not, since that would give him 13 points and he passed as dealer. So you place West with the ace of clubs and hope that the hand will be something like this:

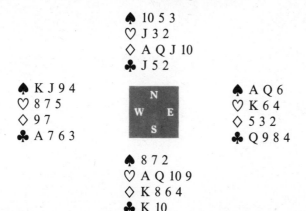

```
                    ♠ 10 5 3
                    ♡ J 3 2
                    ◇ A Q J 10
                    ♣ J 5 2
   ♠ K J 9 4                          ♠ A Q 6
   ♡ 8 7 5              N              ♡ K 6 4
   ◇ 9 7            W       E          ◇ 5 3 2
   ♣ A 7 6 3            S              ♣ Q 9 8 4
                    ♠ 8 7 2
                    ♡ A Q 10 9
                    ◇ K 8 6 4
                    ♣ K 10
```

Scoring 140 may or may not be a good result. At least you will have tried.

20. *Managing a Two-suiter*

In a pairs event less than half the field achieved a plus score on the North–South cards below. Six hearts is unlucky. Six notrumps is a possibility after a diamond lead, because West has awkward discards on the spades. The interesting contract is six spades.

Dealer South   Love all

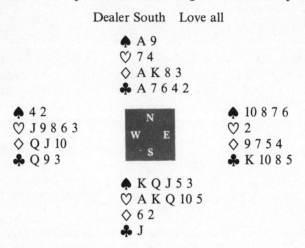

♠ A 9
♡ 7 4
◇ A K 8 3
♣ A 7 6 4 2

♠ 4 2
♡ J 9 8 6 3
◇ Q J 10
♣ Q 9 3

♠ 10 8 7 6
♡ 2
◇ 9 7 5 4
♣ K 10 8 5

♠ K Q J 5 3
♡ A K Q 10 5
◇ 6 2
♣ J

Saying that the bidding begins:

South	North
1♠	2♣
2♡	3◇
3♡	?

At this point 3NT by North would be feeble. He might bid four spades or he might bid just three spades for the moment. This would be forcing after his bid of the fourth suit at the three-level. In any case it should not be difficult to arrive at six spades.

A trump lead may beat this contract if the defenders keep their heads, but West is likely to begin with the queen of diamonds. Now the declarer has an opportunity to display good technique. He leads a heart to the ace, crosses to the ace of clubs and leads a second heart from the table. This is a standard safety play to guard against a 5–1 break in the side suit. It would be poor play for East to ruff the loser. He discards and South wins with the king. The position is now:

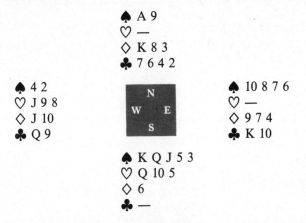

If South leads a low heart and ruffs with the 9, East will overruff and return a trump, leaving South with a losing heart. It is better play to ruff a heart with the ace of spades, cash the king of diamonds, and ruff a club. Now we are down to:

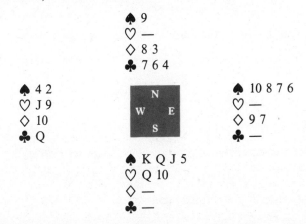

The 10 of hearts is ruffed by the 9 of spades. What can East do? If he overruffs, the rest of South's hand is high; and if he discards, then South will ruff a diamond and make three top trumps.

21. *All Clear*

The deal below is a little out of touch with the rest of this book, because it contains good card reading and a dramatic finish. But it is instructive in its way and not difficult to follow.

Dealer East   E–W vulnerable

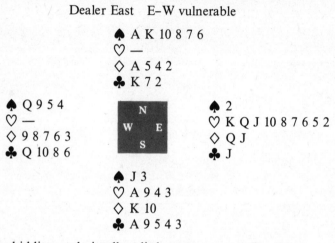

♠ A K 10 8 7 6
♡ —
◇ A 5 4 2
♣ K 7 2

♠ Q 9 5 4
♡ —
◇ 9 8 7 6 3
♣ Q 10 8 6

♠ 2
♡ K Q J 10 8 7 6 5 2
◇ Q J
♣ J

♠ J 3
♡ A 9 4 3
◇ K 10
♣ A 9 5 4 3

The bidding—admittedly a little strange—goes like this:

South	West	North	East
—	—	—	4♡
No	No	4♠	No
6NT (1)	No	No	No

(1) This, obviously, is on the optimistic side. North might have had less. The advantage of playing in notrumps is that the king of diamonds is protected against an opening lead from East. (There is much to be said for playing 4NT as natural, not Blackwood, in all sequences after a pre-emptive opening.)

West leads the 9 of diamonds to the jack and king. If the spades can be picked up without loss there will be eleven tricks on top and normally it would not be difficult to organize a squeeze against West, who is sure to have length in diamonds and clubs. But South, as the cards lie, needs two entries to pick up the spades and the void opposite the ace of hearts is a problem.

South begins by leading the jack of spades, covered by the queen and king. He comes back to hand with a club to the ace, and by this time the distribution is clear. West must be void in hearts, so East's remaining cards are nine hearts and the queen of diamonds.

South finesses the 6 of spades with confidence and runs the spade winners to arrive at this position:

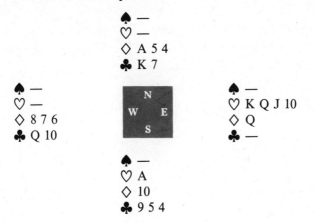

Now a *low* diamond to East's queen, and East has to lead a heart to South's ace. Awkward for West!

PART II—BIDDING TACTICS

At rubber bridge ask your partner what he wants to play—and agree with him unless he suggests some oddity with which you are unfamiliar and which you might forget.

In tournament play the important thing is to play a system you both understand well. You must be able to speak the same language as your partner; if he speaks Chinese and you Spanish, conversation will be difficult. Don't be misled into playing cute variations or seeking to put everything into the pot. On the day when we were composing this advice we read of this sequence in a world championship match:

1♡   2♣
2♠   4♢

Four diamonds meant something or other and you might have thought: 'What a good idea, let's play that.' But it might be a year before the same situation arose, and who is to say that one or other of the partnership won't have forgotten it by then?

The finest buildings start with a ground plan and move slowly upwards. That is the way to build a partnership.

22. *Jump To It*

The North-South hands below are of a type often included in the bidding competitions that appear in the magazines. Seven hearts is on for North–South, but it is not easy to get there, even with the aid of diamond intervention by East–West; not easy, at any rate, when the South hand declines to jump on the first round.

Dealer East   N–S vulnerable

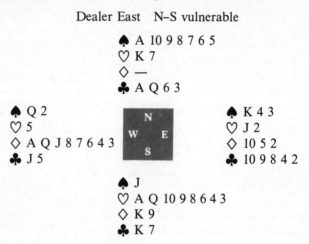

In the final of Australia's principal team event this was the bidding at the first table, where the experienced combination of Norma and Jim Borin held the North–South cards:

South	West	North	East
N. Borin		J. Borin	
—	—	1♠	No
2♡ (1)	3◇	4♣	No
4♡	No	4♠ (2)	No
No (3)	No	No	

(1) Forcing responses have gone out of fashion. Powerful hands of this kind are very difficult to express at all well unless the responder jumps on the first round.

(2) Obviously he might have done something different now, such as five diamonds or five hearts.

(3) South's problem is that she doesn't know about that extremely important card, the king of hearts.

At the other table South did jump on the first round and the result was better, if not perfect:

South	West	North	East
—	—	1♠	No
3♡	4♢	5♢	No
6♡	No	No	No

What, if anything, was wrong with this sequence? North must have fancied the chances of a grand slam, but he has already made a strong bid, five diamonds, and his heart holding is not remarkable. Also, there might possibly be a loser in the spade suit, partner holding something like Q x.

The key to the grand slam lies in North's action over four diamonds. Not knowing at this point whether partner's force is based on strong hearts or on spade support, he should *pass* for the moment. The sequence will then be something like this:

South	West	North	East
—	—	1♠	No
3♡	4♢	No	No
4♡	No	5♣	No
6♡	No	7♡	No
No	No		

South's jump to six hearts shows that there is no duplication in diamonds. If by any chance South has a loser in spades then he will surely hold the king of clubs and there will still be an excellent play for the grand slam.

23. *Forecast Variable*

'Five diamonds is on, but they'll all play in 3NT and go down,' said one of the commentators when this deal appeared on the screen during the semi-finals of the 1987 Bermuda Bowl and Venice Cup. He was right in one sense, but not in the other.

Dealer North   Game all

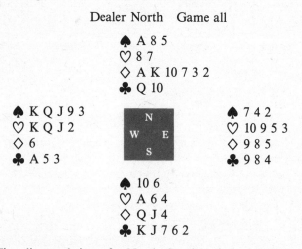

```
              ♠ A 8 5
              ♡ 8 7
              ◇ A K 10 7 3 2
              ♣ Q 10
♠ K Q J 9 3                    ♠ 7 4 2
♡ K Q J 2        N             ♡ 10 9 5 3
◇ 6           W     E          ◇ 9 8 5
♣ A 5 3          S             ♣ 9 8 4
              ♠ 10 6
              ♡ A 6 4
              ◇ Q J 4
              ♣ K J 7 6 2
```

Five diamonds is on for North–South and also, as the cards lie, five clubs against a spade lead. However, hands of this type are usually played in 3NT. Let's look at the various auctions. First, Table 1 in the Bermuda Bowl, Britain v. Sweden:

South	West	North	East
Armstrong	Lindkvist	Kirby	Fallenius
—	—	1NT	No
3NT	Dble	No	No
4♣	No	No	No

When the hand that is not on lead doubles 3NT, this is generally a request for a spade lead, or at any rate for a short suit. South took a good view in running to clubs. Five made, 150 to North–South.

At the other table of this match:

South	West	North	East
Gullberg	Brock	Göthe	Forrester
—	—	No	No
1♣	1♠	2◇	No
2♠	Dble	Redble	No
2NT	No	3NT	No
No	No		

North's original pass denoted opening-bid values. Spade lead, one down, a swing of 6 IMP to Britain.

In the other semi-final, USA v Taipei, the Chinamen played in 3NT one down from the South side, while the Americans made 3NT from the North side against a heart lead; 12 IMP to the USA.

This was USA 1 v. USA 2 in the Venice Cup (the women's championship):

South	West	North	East
Sachs	Palmer	Morse	Deas
—	—	1◇	No
2NT	No	3NT	No
No	Dble	No	No
4♣	No	4◇	No
No	No		

This was similar to Britain v. Sweden, except that North removed four clubs to four diamonds. Eleven tricks, 150 to N–S.

At the other table of this match South made the same response of 2NT to the opening one diamond. West doubled but didn't when North went to 3NT. One down, a swing of 6 IMP to USA 1.

Finally, France v. Italy. When Italy was North–South the bidding to 3NT was the same as in Taipei v. USA. Capodanno, in 3NT, made the correct play of winning the first spade but had to go one down. At the other table Chevalley, for France, *ducked* the spade lead, whereupon West switched to the king of hearts. The declarer won and played off six rounds of diamonds, in the course of which East most unwisely parted with a heart (to give you the count, partner). Now the pressure was too much for West. Contract made, 12 IMP to France.

24. *Not Judging by Results*

For chess players the best age, so they say, is from about 23 to 30, when the brain is at its keenest. Bridge players, on the other hand, seldom reach their best before the mid-thirties and many continue to play well for long after that. Bridge is a many-sided game and experience counts for a great deal. It is interesting that young players are much more subject to fatigue than their elders, who in so many situations 'have been there before'.

Oddly enough, the difference shows more in bidding than in play. Look at this deal from a match between Holland, the eventual winners, and the USA in the 1987 World Junior Championship:

Dealer East   N–S vulnerable

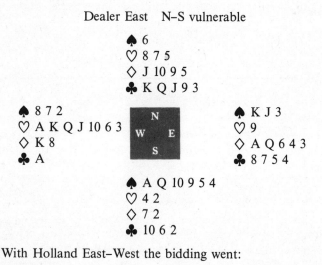

```
                    ♠ 6
                    ♡ 8 7 5
                    ◇ J 10 9 5
                    ♣ K Q J 9 3
  ♠ 8 7 2                          ♠ K J 3
  ♡ A K Q J 10 6 3                 ♡ 9
  ◇ K 8                            ◇ A Q 6 4 3
  ♣ A                              ♣ 8 7 5 4
                    ♠ A Q 10 9 5 4
                    ♡ 4 2
                    ◇ 7 2
                    ♣ 10 6 2
```

With Holland East–West the bidding went:

South	West	North	East
—	—	—	No
2♠ (1)	Dble (2)	No	No (3)
No			

(1) Not an attractive choice, second in hand, vulnerable, but it must be admitted that some experienced players would do the same.

(2) Ridiculous, in preference to four hearts.

(3) If partner had made a take-out double with a singleton spade this pass might have turned out very badly. Best is 2NT, not a weak bid in this sequence.

You will see that we are not judging by results when we criticize the East–West bidding. Everything went very well for the defenders. West cashed the ace of hearts and the ace of clubs, then played the 10 of hearts, encouraging his partner to ruff. A club return was ruffed by West, leaving:

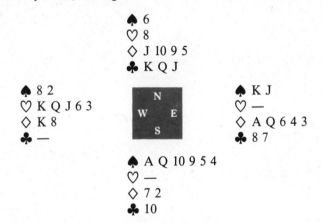

```
                    ♠ 6
                    ♡ 8
                    ◇ J 10 9 5
                    ♣ K Q J

  ♠ 8 2                              ♠ K J
  ♡ K Q J 6 3          N            ♡ —
  ◇ K 8            W       E        ◇ A Q 6 4 3
  ♣ —                  S            ♣ 8 7

                    ♠ A Q 10 9 5 4
                    ♡ —
                    ◇ 7 2
                    ♣ 10
```

West now led the king of diamonds and East overtook with the ace. Another club was ruffed, followed by a diamond to the queen and a fourth club. A dispirited South ruffed low, so West overruffed and East still made the king of spades. This was 1100 and a swing of 12 IMP to the Dutch, who had conceded 420 at the other table.

25. All's Well That Ends Well

This is another deal from the 1987 World Junior Championship.
The story is much the same as in the previous example: moderate
bidding by the Dutch team, then some good play and a bad error
by the Indonesian defender.

Dealer South   E–W vulnerable

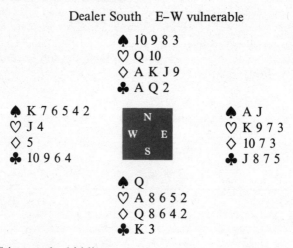

```
                    ♠ 10 9 8 3
                    ♡ Q 10
                    ◇ A K J 9
                    ♣ A Q 2
♠ K 7 6 5 4 2            N            ♠ A J
♡ J 4              W          E       ♡ K 9 7 3
◇ 5                     S            ◇ 10 7 3
♣ 10 9 6 4                           ♣ J 8 7 5
                    ♠ Q
                    ♡ A 8 6 5 2
                    ◇ Q 8 6 4 2
                    ♣ K 3
```

This was the bidding:

South	West	North	East
1♡ (1)	No	1♠ (2)	No
2◇	No	3♣	No
3NT	No	4◇	No
4♡ (3)	No	5♣	No
6◇ (4)	No	No	No

(1) It has become the fashion to open light with two-suiters, but
here the suits themselves are weak and the spade queen may be
worth nothing.

(2) With a strong hand it is usually a mistake to make the first response in a very poor suit; but nowadays, of course, players follow silly rules such as 'Always show a four-card major at the one-level'.

(3) Perhaps the system required him to show a primary control at this point. It seems more sensible to make the weakest available call, five diamonds.

(4) Seeming to forget that he opened the bidding on a weak hand with two empty suits.

The Indonesian West did well to find an opening spade lead against six diamonds. East won the ace and returned the jack, which South ruffed.

Prospects seem poor now, but the Dutch declarer, Leufkens, took his best practical chance by crossing to dummy and leading the queen of hearts. Technically, it is slightly better to lay down the ace with this combination, gaining against a singleton king in either hand, but leading the queen gains when East fails to cover with such as K x x or K x x x. Which is what happened here. Of course, this was very poor play by the defender, because if South has such as A J x x x he will have no problem in establishing the suit without loss.

Maybe it was not so easy to stay short of the slam on this hand. The king of hearts instead of the queen would make it an excellent proposition. If South passes and North opens one diamond, South will force with two hearts. In a bidding competition maybe half the field would finish in six.

26. *Not Fatal*

Everyone hates to double opponents into game at rubber bridge, but the real loss is no more than letting them make a part score when you could have outbid them. You don't believe it? Well, compare two sets of figures. Suppose (a) that you double opponents into game, presenting them, say, with 670 instead of 60 below. Since the part score at game all has an equity value of at least 150, your double has cost about 460. Now suppose (b) that you let opponents make 60 below when you could have outbid them and scored 90 below; the loss now is 150 plus twice the equity value of the part score, a total of 450. A fine player at rubber bridge, Edward Mayer, used to say that if you didn't double opponents into game three or four times a week you weren't doubling enough. Which is interesting.

If your side is going to make borderline doubles in match play it helps if you can defend well. Study this example:

Dealer South   Game all

             ♠ Q 9 5 2
             ♡ 7 3
             ◇ 6 4
             ♣ K Q 8 7 3

♠ A 4   ♠ 8 7
♡ A K 8 4   ♡ Q 9 6 2
◇ K 10 7 3   ◇ J 8 2
♣ A 10 4   ♣ J 9 6 5

             ♠ K J 10 6 3
             ♡ J 10 5
             ◇ A Q 9 5
             ♣ 2

The bidding went:

South	West	North	East
1♠	Dble	3♠	No
No	Dble	No	No
No			

West's second double was borderline. East had a close choice whether to pass rather than attempt a contract at the four level.

West began with two top hearts and led a third round, forcing dummy to ruff. This was good play, since North's club suit was threatening. South played a spade to the king and ace, and West exited with his second trump. South now led his singleton club and West played low—it would have been poor play to go in with the ace. South led a diamond to the 9 and 10, leading to this position:

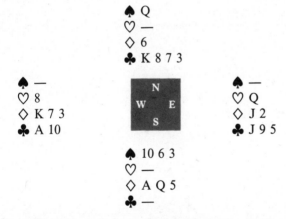

```
                  ♠ Q
                  ♡ —
                  ◇ 6
                  ♣ K 8 7 3
    ♠ —                          ♠ —
    ♡ 8          N               ♡ Q
    ◇ K 7 3   W     E            ◇ J 2
    ♣ A 10       S               ♣ J 9 5
                  ♠ 10 6 3
                  ♡ —
                  ◇ A Q 5
                  ♣ —
```

Now West conceded a ruff-and-discard by leading a fourth heart. As you can see, it was the only play to defeat the contract. (It is almost always right to make this kind of play rather than concede a trick by leading into a tenace.)

So East–West scored 200. As we said above, close doubles call for expert defence.

27. Open Door

Suppose that a vulnerable opponent on your right opens one heart after two passes and you hold:

♠ A K 10 8 6 4
♡ 8 7
◇ —
♣ Q 10 8 5 2

What action do you take? You might overcall one spade, expecting a good tactical result if your partner could raise at any point. You might overcall with an 'intermediate' two spades, the strong distribution compensating for the moderate strength in high cards. You might plunge into four spades. You might fancy one of those two-suited-overcalls; for example, two hearts over one heart would indicate at least five spades and a five-card minor.

In the 1987 Venice Cup, the women's world championship, the American South overcalled with two hearts, the French player bid four spades. See how these calls worked out.

Dealer West   E–W vulnerable

♠ J 5
♡ K Q 10 2
◇ 10 7 3 2
♣ K J 6

♠ 9 3 2   ♠ Q 7
♡ J 5   ♡ A 9 6 4 3
◇ Q 9 5 4   ◇ A K J 8 6
♣ A 9 7 3   ♣ 4

♠ A K 10 8 6 4
♡ 8 7
◇ —
♣ Q 10 8 5 2

The U.S. ladies allowed their opponents to find the diamond fit when the bidding went:

South	West	North	East
—	No	No	1♡
2♡ (1)	No	2NT (2)	3◇
No (3)	5◇	No	No
No			

(1) Showing the two-suiter.

(2) Forcing for the moment, asking partner to name her minor.

(3) South can hardly bid four clubs now, and it wouldn't have helped her side.

Five diamonds was one down, 100 away. This was an optimum result, because five spades by North–South is defeated by a heart lead and a club switch.

At the other table France's Sylvie Willard earned a useful swing for her team by following more direct methods.

South	West	North	East
—	No	No	1♡
4♠	No	No	No

When East won the first trick with the ace of hearts she tried a high diamond, so that was 450 to France and a swing of 8 match points.

When Willard was asked how she came to risk a four spade overcall, she replied:

'As West and North both passed and East opened with a bid of one, I thought the missing cards would be fairly equally divided. I would never treat my hand as a two-suiter. If I had bid simply two spades West would have made a negative double and they would have gone to five diamonds over four spades.'

Yes, there was good sense in that.

28. *Not Impressed*

In the 1987 Lederer Cup the team described as 'England', containing two relatively unfamiliar partnerships, finished second to the Swedish holders of the European Championship, ahead of many more practised formations. On the following deal Sandra Landy and John Pottage, playing a natural system, reached a slam that was missed by the majority.

Dealer North   Love all

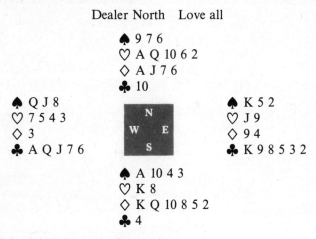

```
                    ♠ 9 7 6
                    ♡ A Q 10 6 2
                    ◇ A J 7 6
                    ♣ 10
  ♠ Q J 8                              ♠ K 5 2
  ♡ 7 5 4 3            N               ♡ J 9
  ◇ 3               W     E            ◇ 9 4
  ♣ A Q J 7 6          S               ♣ K 9 8 5 3 2
                    ♠ A 10 4 3
                    ♡ K 8
                    ◇ K Q 10 8 5 2
                    ♣ 4
```

This was their successful auction:

South	West	North	East
—	—	1♡	No
2◇	No	3◇	No
3♠	No	5◇	No
6◇	No	No	No

The North–South hands contained only 23 points between them and there was not even a good fit, both players having the same singleton. If South had held a club more and a spade less, the slam would have been a better proposition. As it was, the declarer needed to develop five tricks in hearts.

West cashed the ace of clubs and switched to the queen of spades. The play seemed to proceed without incident. South won with the ace of spades and played off six rounds of diamonds, on which West discarded four clubs and one heart. The declarer then cashed king and ace of hearts and had twelve tricks when the jack appeared.

This was the result at other tables, too, where South was in six diamonds. Perhaps the West players were a trifle slow-witted. It is soon evident that South is hoping to make five tricks in hearts. (If his spades had been A K x x he would have needed only four tricks from hearts and would not have removed the trump entry.) West should have clung to his hearts, so that the end position would be:

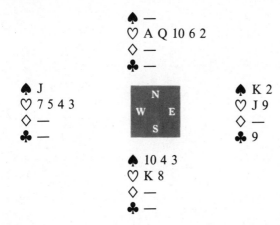

                ♠ —
                ♡ A Q 10 6 2
                ◇ —
                ♣ —

    ♠ J   ♠ K 2
    ♡ 7 5 4 3   N   ♡ J 9
    ◇ —   W   E   ◇ —
    ♣ —   S   ♣ 9

                ♠ 10 4 3
                ♡ K 8
                ◇ —
                ♣ —

When South played the king of hearts, followed by the 8, he would have pondered for a long while whether to finesse the 10, playing West for J x x x. He would not, of course, be impressed by East's 9 on the first round, which could easily be from 9 x.

29. Count Five

While rubber bridge players, in general, use Blackwood simply as an inquiry for aces, most tournament players use some form of five–ace Blackwood, in which the king of the proposed trump suit (or, in some versions, any important king) is assigned the same value as an ace; then a response of five hearts to 4NT shows two such aces, five spades two aces and a critical king or three aces. Playing this method, you can avoid finishing in a slam when you are missing an ace and the king of trumps. The hazard involved in playing simple Blackwood was evident on this deal from the Philip Morris Europa Cup:

Dealer North   Game all

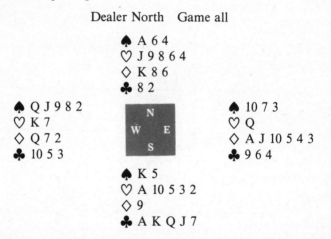

♠ A 6 4
♡ J 9 8 6 4
◇ K 8 6
♣ 8 2

♠ Q J 9 8 2
♡ K 7
◇ Q 7 2
♣ 10 5 3

♠ 10 7 3
♡ Q
◇ A J 10 5 4 3
♣ 9 6 4

♠ K 5
♡ A 10 5 3 2
◇ 9
♣ A K Q J 7

When a British pair was North–South against Austrian opponents, the bidding went like this:

South	West	North	East
Whittleton	Fucik	Dempster	Kubak
—	—	No	No
1♡	No	3♡	No
4♣	No	4♡	No
4♠ (1)	No	6♡ (2)	No
No	No		

(1) This second try seems doubtful. It wasn't likely that his partner would hold an ace and the K Q of hearts, so a slam could hardly be lay-down.

(2) This was certainly justified after his previous sign-off.

West led the queen of spades to dummy's ace. The declarer cashed the ace of hearts, then followed with ace and jack of clubs. West naturally ruffed the fourth round of clubs and the defence was in time to cash the setting trick in diamonds.

A Danish reporter in the Bulletin of the International Bridge Press Association remarked 'Amazingly, South did not try to fool his opponents.' Do you see what he had in mind?

South's only chance is somehow to dispose of all three diamonds from dummy by the time that West has ruffed. His best play is to begin with ace, king and queen of clubs, arriving at this position:

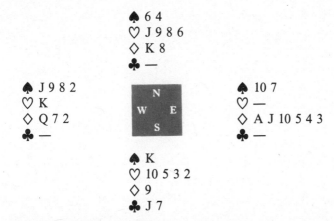

Now South leads the 7 of clubs . . . and if West is dreaming and thinks his partner holds the jack he may fail to ruff.

At the other table of this match the Austrians employed five-ace Blackwood, stopped in time, and gained 13 IMP. In the same way, Sweden gained 13 against Belgium.

30. *Fear the Worst*

In pairs events, especially, it does not pay to be an optimist at bridge. When you are not sure whether or not to try for a slam, consider (a) what might happen at the five level and (b) whether your partner will know what the problems are and will be in a position to make a sensible decision. Many pairs went too high on this deal from a pairs contest:

Dealer South   Game all

```
                ♠ K J 5 2
                ♡ Q 9 4 2
                ◊ A Q 7
                ♣ J 4
♠ Q 9 8 7 4                        ♠ —
♡ K 10 6 3                         ♡ A J 8 5
◊ K 6 4                            ◊ J 10 9 5 3 2
♣ 2                               ♣ 10 8 3
                ♠ A 10 6 3
                ♡ 7
                ◊ 8
                ♣ A K Q 9 7 6 5
```

At several tables the bidding began on these lines:

South	North
1♣	1♡
1♠	4♠
?	

Now the South hand was difficult to value. If partner held ♠ K Q x x and one of the red aces, or ♠ K x x x and two aces, then six spades would be a good contract. However, it is not sound to plunge into 4NT or raise to five spades. There are too many hands where five spades might be uncomfortable. Also, partner might not be sure exactly what was required of him.

The majority did pass four spades, but owing to the bad trump break even this proved difficult. Suppose that West leads his singleton club and that South wins in dummy and leads a low spade towards the A 10 x x. When East shows out, South puts in the 10, not wanting to release his sure entry. Now a good player in West's position will win with the spade queen and lead the king of hearts, followed by the 10. South ruffs and tries the queen of clubs. When West ruffs this and leads a third heart, the contract becomes impossible.

Admittedly, this is unlucky as you won't often run into a 5–0 break. But the play was wrong. South is aiming to set up his own hand and on general principles should begin with the king of spades from dummy. So long as everyone follows to this, the play will be easy. In practice, East shows out. Now South plays on clubs. West ruffs the second round and attacks in hearts, as before. This is the situation after South has ruffed the second heart:

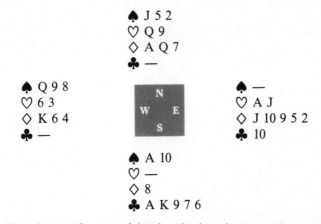

```
                    ♠ J 5 2
                    ♡ Q 9
                    ◊ A Q 7
                    ♣ —
    ♠ Q 9 8                          ♠ —
    ♡ 6 3          N                 ♡ A J
    ◊ K 6 4     W     E              ◊ J 10 9 5 2
    ♣ —            S                 ♣ 10
                    ♠ A 10
                    ♡ —
                    ◊ 8
                    ♣ A K 9 7 6
```

West has made two tricks, but he is going to make only one more. South leads a high club and West, perhaps, will ruff with the queen and lead another heart. No matter; South ruffs with ♠ 10 and repeats the dose by continuing clubs.

31. *No Distinction*

It is advisable, on the whole, to have some way of distinguishing between distributional raises to game and 'value' raises, usually expressed by four clubs, or four diamonds. North–South reached an unsafe contract on this deal from rubber bridge, and I don't see that South could be blamed.

Dealer South   N–S vulnerable

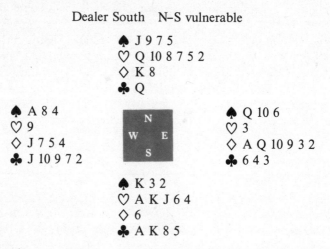

♠ J 9 7 5
♡ Q 10 8 7 5 2
◇ K 8
♣ Q

♠ A 8 4
♡ 9
◇ J 7 5 4
♣ J 10 9 7 2

♠ Q 10 6
♡ 3
◇ A Q 10 9 3 2
♣ 6 4 3

♠ K 3 2
♡ A K J 6 4
◇ 6
♣ A K 8 5

South opened one heart and North raised to four hearts. South applied the 'old Black'—can you blame him—and the partnership subsided in five hearts.

The hands did not fit well, and this was not a comfortable contract. As the play went, it depended on the position of the ♠8!

South won the club lead in dummy, drew trumps and hastily discarded two diamonds from dummy on ♣ A K. After a diamond ruff, a trump, and a club ruff he arrived at this position:

```
                    ♠ J 9 7 5
                    ♡ Q
                    ◇ —
                    ♣ —

♠ A 8 4                              ♠ Q 10 6
♡ —            ┌─────────┐           ♡ —
◇ J 7          │    N    │           ◇ A Q
♣ —            │  W   E  │           ♣ —
               │    S    │
               └─────────┘
                    ♠ K 3 2
                    ♡ J 6
                    ◇ —
                    ♣ —
```

It wasn't obvious now whether South should lead the 7 of spades or the 9 from dummy. He could afford to lose two tricks in spades and if West held the 10, then the 9 would be a sure winner. There doesn't seem to be much in it. South in practice led the 7 and let it run to West's 8. There was nothing the defence could do now.

Disappointed by this turn of events, one of the defenders said, 'You were lucky to find the spades the way you did. Isn't it better to throw spades on the top clubs? Then you always make it when I (West) have the ace of diamonds, and if not, you can still play my partner for the ace of spades.'

Perhaps; but this line may require the same defender to hold both aces, which is always slightly against the odds.

32. *Losing Policy*

The method of valuation known as the Losing Trick Count is seldom mentioned nowadays, and neither of the present authors was ever a great supporter. Nevertheless, it contained an essential truth in the sense that tricks are won and lost by playing values, not by the presence or absence of 'points', which are so prominent in the teaching of bridge. As an example of what we mean, consider the way the South hand below was valued by the players who held it in a pairs event.

Dealer North   Game all

```
              ♠ K 7 6 2
              ♡ A 9 5
              ◇ K Q 4 2
              ♣ 9 3
♠ J 9 8                        ♠ Q 10
♡ K Q J 7                      ♡ 10 4 3
◇ A J 9 5      N               ◇ 10 8
♣ 10 6       W   E             ♣ Q 8 7 5 4 2
               S
              ♠ A 5 4 3
              ♡ 8 6 2
              ◇ 7 6 3
              ♣ A K J
```

Almost every pair reached four spades, generally with this kind of sequence:

South	West	North	East
—	—	1◇	No
1♠	No	2♠	No
3♣	No	3♠	No
4♠	No	No	No

South is just about entitled to make one game try. If partner has only three spades and perhaps 3–3–5–2 distribution, then 3NT may be a fair contract. But four spades when he has signed off in three spades? There you see the effect of bad teaching. 'I had 12 points', they say, or 'I had three-plus quick tricks'. But how many losers?

For four spades to be on, after a heart lead, South needs the club finesse to establish a discard, ace of diamonds on the right side, and spades 3–2. Oddly enough, all these happy events existed, but still only one pair at seven tables was able to record +620. It's not quite so easy as it may look.

South wins the second trick with the ace of hearts and should finesse the jack of clubs to establish a discard. This wins, so he follows with ace and king of clubs. West intervenes with a ruff, but luckily it is from three trumps and the third heart is discarded from dummy, according to plan. Now West is on lead in this position:

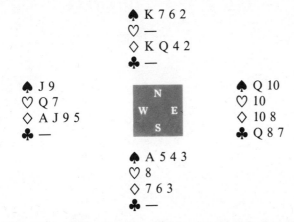

```
                    ♠ K 7 6 2
                    ♡ —
                    ◇ K Q 4 2
                    ♣ —
    ♠ J 9                              ♠ Q 10
    ♡ Q 7              N               ♡ 10
    ◇ A J 9 5       W     E            ◇ 10 8
    ♣ —                S               ♣ Q 8 7
                    ♠ A 5 4 3
                    ♡ 8
                    ◇ 7 6 3
                    ♣ —
```

West exists with a heart, ruffed by dummy's 2 of spades. South plays king and another spade, then a diamond to the king. All has gone well, except that South has no entry back to hand for another diamond lead. He tries a low diamond from dummy, but West overtakes his partner's 10 and cashes the ace to defeat the contract.

If only South had ruffed the third heart with dummy's 6 of spades instead of the 2 he would have had another entry back to hand and would have made the luckiest of game contracts.

33. *A Question of Tactics*

The deal below, from a ladies' match between France and Italy in the European Championship, contained some tricky bidding problems. Suppose, first, that as dealer at game all you pick up:

♠ A 7 6 4
♡ 10 9 7 6 5 3
♢ K Q
♣ 9

Forget the old-fashioned 2½ honour tricks, and don't be guided by point count. What are the advantages of opening one heart? First, the arguments against:

(1) On certain occasions when partner has fair values but a singleton heart, the hand will prove awkward; but this won't be too bad if, in the Acol style, you play a sequence such as one heart—2NT—three hearts as non-forcing.

(2) If opponents obtain the contract you may cause partner to make the wrong opening lead. At notrumps the heart lead may not be bad, but in a suit call there is the danger that he may start with the king from such as K x.

The arguments in favour of opening are:

(1) It will be a useful hand if partner has support in hearts; you may obtain the contract when your side has less than half the high cards.

(2) It is an advantage that your second suit is spades. If you don't open, partner with a spade suit may not be able to enter the bidding.

(3) If your partner supports hearts, but opponents obtain the contract, your honours in the side suits will be useful in defence.

See how those considerations would have operated on the present occasion.

Dealer North   Game all

```
              ♠ A 7 6 4
              ♡ 10 9 7 6 5 3
              ◇ K Q
              ♣ 9
♠ 9 5                        ♠ K J 10 3 2
♡ A 8 2          N           ♡ —
◇ A J 10 5    W     E        ◇ 8 7 3
♣ 10 5 4 3       S           ♣ K Q 8 7 2
              ♠ Q 8
              ♡ K Q J 4
              ◇ 9 6 4 2
              ♣ A J 6
```

The French North opened one heart and played in four hearts without much opposition. There were just three losers in this contract. This was the bidding at the other table:

South	West	North	East
—	—	No	No
1♡	No	4♣ (1)	Dble (2)
4♡	No	No	4♠ (3)
No	5♣	5♡ (4)	No
No	Dble	No	No
No			

(1) For some players this type of response is 'Swiss', showing good values; for others, it is a 'splinter', indicating shortage in the suit named.

(2) Either way, East has a good double. Such doubles sometimes attract a good lead, sometimes prepare a sacrifice.

(3) Interesting! East, in effect, is showing a black two-suiter.

(4) Is this right? True, she has fine support for her partner's one heart opening, but also she has at least two tricks outside.

South was one down in five hearts doubled, so there was a swing of 12 match points to the French, who went on to win the championship.

[77]

34. *Sputnik Style*

Many of the country's best players developed their talents at the universities, but to watch the annual Oxford v. Cambridge match for the Waddington Cup is still a frightening experience. For one thing, the players tend to be exceedingly slow, and for another, they seek to incorporate all the latest complexities in their game. Concentration is a very important factor in bridge, and players who need to think deeply about every bid and play tend to make silly mistakes on simple hands. Study the events on this deal from the 1987 university match:

Dealer North   N–S vulnerable

```
                    ♠ K 5
                    ♡ A K Q 7 6 5
                    ◇ 8 7
                    ♣ 5 4 2
   ♠ J 10 6 2                        ♠ 8
   ♡ 9 8 4                           ♡ 10 3
   ◇ K 10 3                          ◇ Q 9 5 4
   ♣ A 10 7                          ♣ K Q J 9 6 3
                    ♠ A Q 9 7 4 3
                    ♡ J 2
                    ◇ A J 6 2
                    ♣ 8
```

This was the bidding when Oxford held the North–South cards:

South	West	North	East
—	—	1♡	2♣
Dble (1)	No	2♡	No
2♠ (2)	No	No (3)	No

(1) If you are playing negative (sputnik) doubles, it is not wrong here to make what is known as a high-powered double, with the intention of bidding again on the next round.

(2) This sequence, in the modern style, is forcing. An immediate two spades on the preceding round would *not* have been forcing.

(3) But North had either forgotten or had not been reading the same book (namely, *Bridge—The Modern Game*, by Terence Reese and David Bird).

South made eleven tricks, +200. Whether this would be a good result or not was likely to depend on the early play at the other table. The Cambridge pair in fact reached the best slam contract, six hearts. It looks as though this will be defeated by a club lead and a diamond switch, removing the entry for the long spades.

However, East led his singleton spade against six hearts, a terrible choice, since there was no possibility at all of finding his partner with the ace of spades. Such leads are capable of killing partner's Q x x or J x x x, and here of course there was an excellent alternative.

Nothing could have been easier for declarer, after the spade lead, than to draw trumps and set up the spades, with the ace of diamonds for entry. He makes six tricks in hearts, five in spades and one in diamonds.

But North, perhaps exhausted by previous efforts, miscounted his tricks. He played a club at trick two. The defenders took their spade ruff and North finished two down. It was a swing of 9 match points to Oxford, despite an inglorious performance at both tables.

35. Catching Up

The South hand below is of a type easier to bid in the one club systems than in Acol or CAB. If you start with a conventional one club you have plenty of time in which to discover that the values are not quite there for a slam—though obviously there are chances in six spades.

At Acol the opening bid is debatable. If you open one spade it will be difficult to express the hand afterwards even if you have the chance. You may open two clubs, intending to rebid 2NT, non-forcing. On the present occasion the CAB method works well. North shows his ace of hearts over two clubs and there is time in which to decide that the combined hands are not quite worth a slam.

Dealer South   N–S vulnerable

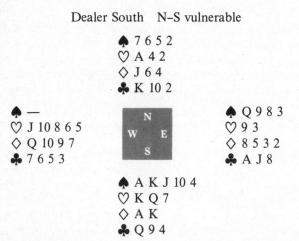

♠ 7 6 5 2
♡ A 4 2
◇ J 6 4
♣ K 10 2

♠ —
♡ J 10 8 6 5
◇ Q 10 9 7
♣ 7 6 5 3

♠ Q 9 8 3
♡ 9 3
◇ 8 5 3 2
♣ A J 8

♠ A K J 10 4
♡ K Q 7
◇ A K
♣ Q 9 4

At rubber bridge South, playing Acol, opened two clubs and the bidding continued:

South	West	North	East
2♣	No	2♢ (1)	No
2♠ (2)	No	3♠	No
4♠	No	4NT	No
5♡	No	5♠ (3)	No
No	No		

(1) It has become a fashion not to respond 2NT on hands where the bid is technically justified. Players have the notion that there will be time to catch up after a negative.

(2) Not really sound, because it is not a game hand if partner is weak. If South is going to begin with two clubs he should rebid 2NT.

(3) By this time it would be more accurate to say, not that North had caught up, but that his first response had caught up with him.

It is not a disgrace to finish at the five level on this hand, but the play proved awkward. West began with the jack of hearts. South won and laid down the ace of spades, discovering the 4–0 break. Hoping to enter dummy twice, he advanced the queen of clubs. East, naturally, looked the other way. Not very happy now, South finessed the 10 of clubs, losing to the jack. East cashed the ace of clubs, then exited with a diamond. South could enter dummy with the ace of hearts but he still had to lose a trump trick and go one down.

'When you found the trumps 4–0, couldn't you have crossed to dummy with a heart, finessed in spades, cashed the top diamonds, then led a club to the king and ace?' North suggested. 'East can exit with a third diamond, but then you play queen and another club and East is end-played.'

'That's double-dummy', South replied, with justification.

No-one pointed out a simpler solution. When he discovers the trump division South should lead the 9 of clubs and run it. East wins with the jack but now there are two entries to dummy for the trump finesses.

36. *That Little Extra*

Suppose that you held the South hand below and your partner had opened 2NT. In tournament play you would probably be using transfer responses. The choice then would be between responding three diamonds, with the idea of playing in six hearts, or leaping to 6NT, which in a pairs event might produce the extra match points.

At rubber bridge, not playing transfer responses, the choice will lie between 6NT and six hearts, with the disadvantage then that the lead will be through partner's strength. The importance of this element is perhaps overestimated; the defenders, generally speaking, will not lead from honour cards into the strong hand, so it will be the *position* of the high cards that will matter, and this will be the same whether North or South is the declarer.

On the present hand North opened 2NT and South, not playing transfers, became the declarer in six hearts. There was an extra chance in this contract, which he overlooked.

Dealer North   Game all

```
                    ♠ A K J
                    ♡ J 10 4
                    ◇ A K 7
                    ♣ A 10 9 2
    ♠ 8 4 2                              ♠ Q 10 9 5
    ♡ 7 5                                ♡ 8 3
    ◇ Q J 10 6 4                         ◇ 9 5 2
    ♣ K Q 8                              ♣ J 7 6 5
                    ♠ 7 6 3
                    ♡ A K Q 9 6 2
                    ◇ 8 3
                    ♣ 4 3
```

The bidding went:

South	West	North	East
—	—	2NT	No
3♡	No	3NT	No
5♡	No	6♡	No
No	No		

South took the reasonable view that if his partner had held tenace positions, such as A Q x or K J x, he could have bid 5NT over five hearts. So South was content to play in the suit contract.

West led a diamond to the king, and after drawing trumps and cashing one high spade South could see nothing better than the spade finesse. So, 100 to the opposition.

In 6NT this result would have been unavoidable, but in six hearts there was the extra chance of finding West with such as K Q x, K J x or Q J x in clubs. After drawing trumps South leads a low club from hand. Say that West splits his honours (it makes no difference). In this case South wins with the ace in dummy, returns to hand and leads another club in this position:

```
                    ♠ A K J
                    ♡ —
                    ◇ A 7
                    ♣ 10 9 2
  ♠ 8 4 2                            ♠ Q 10 9
  ♡ —              ┌───────┐        ♡ —
  ◇ J 10 6         │   N   │        ◇ 9 5
  ♣ K 8           │ W   E │        ♣ J 7 6
                   │   S   │
                    └───────┘
                    ♠ 7 6 3
                    ♡ 9 6 2
                    ◇ 8
                    ♣ 4
```

Whether West plays the 8 of clubs or the king on this trick, it will not be difficult for South to establish a club winner.

You see here the advantage of playing in the suit contract. There are many combinations in a side suit where there may be a chance of establishing an extra trick without risk. For example, A Q 9 x opposite x x, K Q 9 x opposite x x (when the defender sitting over the king–queen holds J 10 x). And with a holding such as A K J x opposite a singleton or doubleton you may, in a suit contract, seek to drop the queen in three rounds before trying in other suits.

37. *Homer Nodded*

To have a big reputation as a player is good in some ways, but it does mean that when you make a mistake—a rather bad one on this occasion—the world gets to know about it. A Danish journalist reported this deal from the match between France and Denmark in a European Championship match.

Dealer South   N–S vulnerable

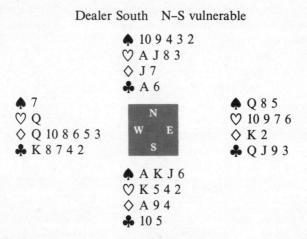

```
                    ♠ 10 9 4 3 2
                    ♡ A J 8 3
                    ◇ J 7
                    ♣ A 6
   ♠ 7                              ♠ Q 8 5
   ♡ Q                              ♡ 10 9 7 6
   ◇ Q 10 8 6 5 3                   ◇ K 2
   ♣ K 8 7 4 2                      ♣ Q J 9 3
                    ♠ A K J 6
                    ♡ K 5 4 2
                    ◇ A 9 4
                    ♣ 10 5
```

The French played in four spades, with no opposition bidding. West led a diamond and the declarer lost a trick in each suit.

At the other table West indicated his minor two-suiter with an overcall of 2NT. It is not a tactic we admire, but many good players do it, especially at favourable vulnerability. The sensible bid for North over 2NT is four spades, but he and his partner bid around the clock and finally went to five spades over East's five clubs. (If North bids four spades on the first round, then with his two outside aces and two doubletons he can double five clubs.)

In view of the 2NT overcall it is easy for South to pick up the queen of spades, and he did so, but there still seem to be three losers. The play went: club to the ace, ace of spades, low heart to the queen and ace, spade finesse and spade king. Now South exited with a club, which West allowed to run to his partner's jack. This left:

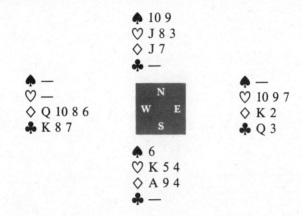

```
              ♠ 10 9
              ♡ J 8 3
              ◇ J 7
              ♣ —
  ♠ —                        ♠ —
  ♡ —          N             ♡ 10 9 7
  ◇ Q 10 8 6  W    E         ◇ K 2
  ♣ K 8 7         S          ♣ Q 3
              ♠ 6
              ♡ K 5 4
              ◇ A 9 4
              ♣ —
```

Chemla, sitting East, exited safely enough with the 10 of hearts, which ran to dummy's jack. Now South led a low diamond from the table and Chemla made a terrible mistake—he played low. When he won the next round of diamonds with the king he was on play: either a heart into the divided tenace or a club would cost a trick. So the declarer made his contract of five spades.

PART III—DEFENSIVE MOVES

'What's the contract? Is it my lead?' Oh dear, if your partner is that sort, change him (or her) as soon as you can.

You must *listen* to the bidding, drawing all the inferences you can, both positive and negative. Form a picture of the declarer's hand even before the dummy goes down. You'll be surprised how close you can get sometimes after quite ordinary sequences.

Against most contracts make the normal, the obvious lead. There are two reasons for this. First, partner will seldom blame you if you make the natural lead—especially when he has entered the bidding and you are leading his suit. Second, in duplicate play it is better to make the same lead as the others and hope to play well afterwards than to risk an unusual lead that may ruin your chances of a good board.

We advised simple bidding and we advise simple play as well. Don't go in for elaborate 'carding'—the refuge of those who have no perception. Signal only in the obvious situations. Trust your partner to know what is happening and don't make it so easy for declarer to read the hand.

38. Through the Slips

It is always a little humiliating, when defending against 3NT, to take a trick in the middle of the play and fail to cash four more that are immediately available. Normally there is some indication pointing to the right play. See what you think of this hand from a team-of-four match.

Dealer West   Game all

                    ♠ K 5
                    ♡ 6
                    ◇ J 9 4
                    ♣ A K J 10 8 3 2

♠ J 10 7 4 3   ♠ Q 9 6 2
♡ A J 8 3   ♡ K Q 4 2
◇ K 2   ◇ 7 5
♣ 9 4   ♣ Q 7 6

                    ♠ A 8
                    ♡ 10 9 7 5
                    ◇ A Q 10 8 6 3
                    ♣ 5

This was the bidding at the first table:

South	West	North	East
—	No	1♣	No
1◇	No	2♣	No
2♡ (1)	No	3♣ (2)	No
3NT (3)	No	No	No

(1) Two diamonds at this point would not have been a sign-off, but South may have thought he was a little too strong.

(2) North's best bid at this point is debatable. He was too good for three clubs, certainly. He might have bid 2NT or raised the diamonds or bid four clubs.

(3) As the bidding had gone, this was optimistic.

West led a low spade, which ran to the queen and ace. The declarer cashed two clubs, then ran the jack of diamonds, losing to West's king. West played another spade and South was home with five diamonds and four top cards in the black suits. 'He had bid hearts', said West. 'How could I possibly switch to a heart?'

If West directs his mind to that question, the answer is not too difficult to find. Declarer's play of the ace and king of clubs is not the normal way to play such a combination. It was plain that he was giving himself two chances (the clubs and the diamonds) to run his tricks before losing the lead.

Looking at it another way, if South had held a heart stopper he would have won the first spade and forced out the queen of clubs. When in doubt, ask yourself what declarer would be doing if he held certain cards. That is what defence is about.

At the other table South did bid only two diamonds on the second round. The bidding went like this:

South	North
—	1♣
1♢	2♣
2♢	3♢
5♢	No

This was a good contract and North–South were unlucky not to gain a swing. South won the spade lead, cashed ace of diamonds, played a club to the ace and ruffed a club with the queen of diamonds. Then he led a low diamond, conceding a trick to the king and scoring 600.

39. *Before They Know*

There is generally a point in the play of a hand when the defenders know more about the distribution of a particular suit than the declarer. It may be possible then to put declarer to a premature guess. Everyone, on occasions, leads from a king through dummy's A Q, hoping that declarer will reject the finesse in favour of another possible chance. On the present deal a defender missed a less obvious play of this kind.

Dealer South   Love all

♠ A 10 8 4 2
♡ J 10
◇ Q 4
♣ A J 6 5

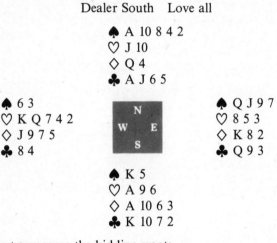

♠ 6 3
♡ K Q 7 4 2
◇ J 9 7 5
♣ 8 4

♠ Q J 9 7
♡ 8 5 3
◇ K 8 2
♣ Q 9 3

♠ K 5
♡ A 9 6
◇ A 10 6 3
♣ K 10 7 2

In a team game the bidding went:

South	West	North	East
1NT	No	2♣	No
2◇	No	3♠ (1)	No
3NT	No	No	No

(1) Tournament players usually make a distinction between a direct jump in a major suit, 1NT–3♠, and a jump following Stayman. Here North's three spades was forcing.

West led a low heart and dummy's jack held the first trick. South began with a spade to the king and a spade back, on which he played the 10 from dummy. East won and a heart to the queen was followed by a third round to South's ace.

The discard from dummy on the third round of hearts called for a little consideration. Since three tricks in spades would be enough for the contract, South discarded a spade from dummy rather than a club.

After winning with the ace of hearts declarer played the king of clubs and low to the jack, finessing towards the safe hand. The position was now:

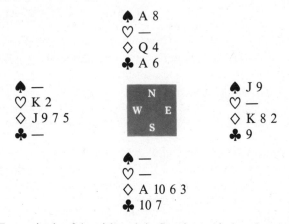

East exited safely with a club. South won in hand, crossed to the ace, and led the ace of spades. The last spade was not a winner, but it was simple to exit with a spade, forcing East to concede the ninth trick by leading from the king of diamonds.

What strikes you about this play? The interesting point is that when in with the queen of clubs East should have exited boldly with the 2 or 8 of diamonds. The odds are that South would have gone up with the ace, hoping for a 3–3 division in spades.

40. *Leading Questions*

Suppose that you hold something like 7 5 2 in partner's suit and intend to lead this suit in a trump contract: do you begin with the 7, the 5 or the 2? This is an area in which fashions have changed considerably over the years.

In the early days it was normal to lead top-of-nothing either in partner's suit or in an unbid suit. Then, for a period, many players favoured the middle card, to be followed by the top card. This style is known as MUD, standing for middle-up-down. Nowadays the Americans, and many European players, generally lead the lowest card from three small.

The idea behind MUD is that if you lead the 5 from 7 5 2 and follow with the 7 partner will know that you hold three, and with such as A K x x x he will not attempt to give you a ruff; but meanwhile playing off the two top cards may prove an egregious error. For this reason, most good players in these days lead the bottom card from three small. It is true that this does not distinguish between, say, 7 5 2 and Q 5 2, but on balance it is more important to give partner an immediate indication of the length.

There is another reason why top-of-nothing may be a mistake. Sometimes the top card is valuable, as on this deal:

Dealer North   Love all

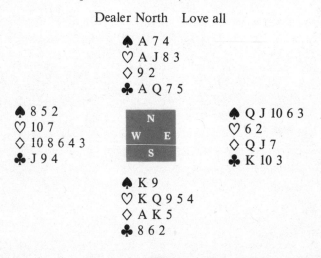

[92]

North–South reach a slam after East has overcalled in spades.

South	West	North	East
—	—	1♣	1♠
2♡	No	4♡	No
4NT	No	5♠	No
6♡	No	No	No

Oddly enough, you may think, the lead of the 8 of spades by West is fatal for the defence. South wins with the king, draws trumps, and eliminates the diamonds, reaching this position:

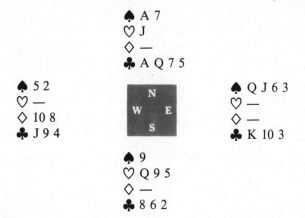

South does not need to be a champion now to play a loser-on-loser elimination: ace and another spade, discarding a club from hand and leaving East on play.

This end-play cannot be achieved if West begins with the 2 of spades instead of the 8. In this case the declarer's best chance will be to eliminate the spades and lead a low club from hand. Let us hope, for the good of his soul, that West is sufficiently awake to insert the 9!

41. *Two for One*

Players don't like to do it, but there are times when with A Q of trumps over the declarer's king it is good play to lead the ace and follow with the queen. The *locus classicus* for this type of play occurred in a Camrose Trophy match between England and Scotland.

Dealer West   N–S vulnerable

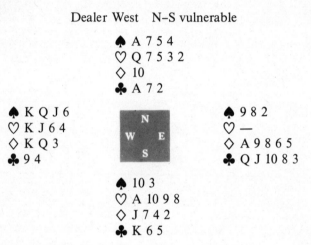

```
                    ♠ A 7 5 4
                    ♡ Q 7 5 3 2
                    ◇ 10
                    ♣ A 7 2
   ♠ K Q J 6                      ♠ 9 8 2
   ♡ K J 6 4          N           ♡ —
   ◇ K Q 3        W       E       ◇ A 9 8 6 5
   ♣ 9 4              S           ♣ Q J 10 8 3
                    ♠ 10 3
                    ♡ A 10 9 8
                    ◇ J 7 4 2
                    ♣ K 6 5
```

Playing five-card majors, West felt constrained to open one diamond in preference to one spade. The bidding continued:

South	West	North	East
—	1◇	2◇ (1)	4◇
4♡	Dble (2)	No	No (3)
No			

(1) The Michaels cue bid, denoting limited values with length in both majors. It turned out well on this occasion because partner had good hearts. Such overcalls are often more helpful to the opposition.

(2) Doubtful; his side will not make more than one trick in diamonds and his hearts may be badly placed.

(3) Many players would take out into five diamonds, but he has as much defence as he has so far suggested and sometimes one's partners know what they are doing.

West made a very good lead—a low trump. It was clear that the opponents were going to play on cross-ruff lines, because West held strong spades and his partner was sure to have length in clubs.

South won with ♡ 8 and led a spade, ducking in dummy when West produced the jack. West continued with ♡ 6. South won with the 9 and led a low diamond, won by West's queen. The position was now:

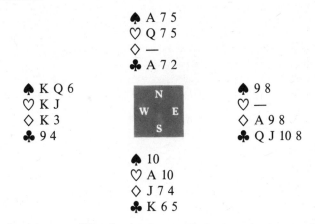

```
                ♠ A 7 5
                ♡ Q 7 5
                ◊ —
                ♣ A 7 2
  ♠ K Q 6                        ♠ 9 8
  ♡ K J          N               ♡ —
  ◊ K 3      W       E           ◊ A 9 8
  ♣ 9 4          S               ♣ Q J 10 8
                ♠ 10
                ♡ A 10
                ◊ J 7 4
                ♣ K 6 5
```

At this stage West broke down. He had made two good leads and it should have been clear that to lead the jack of hearts could not possibly cost. South can win in dummy, but when he ruffs a spade with the ace of hearts West's king will be restored to the throne. South in fact will lose a spade and a heart at the finish.

When West exited with a spade in the diagram position South had a gay time. He won with the ace, ruffed a spade, ruffed a diamond, then played two clubs and ruffed another diamond. Now dummy's fourth spade was ruffed by the ace of hearts and the fourth diamond established a trick for dummy's queen of hearts.

42. *Cut and Run*

What used to be called the 'Coup Without a Name' now has a name—the Scissors Coup. The idea is that the declarer averts a ruff by cutting the enemy communications. In books and articles the declarer's plan always succeeds, but this was a time when the defenders played too well for him.

Dealer West   Game all

♠ 4
♡ K Q 10 7 3
♢ K 10 6 5
♣ 10 9 2

♠ A 7
♡ J 9 4
♢ 7 3
♣ A Q J 8 6 4

♠ K 5 2
♡ 8 6
♢ Q J 9 8 4 2
♣ 7 3

♠ Q J 10 9 8 6 3
♡ A 5 2
♢ A
♣ K 5

The bidding went:

South	West	North	East
—	1♣	No (1)	1♢
2♠	No	3♡ (2)	No
4♠	No	No	No

(1) North has minimum, or sub-minimum, strength for a vulnerable overcall and is right to take into consideration that one heart may not deprive the opponents of any bidding space. If the spades and hearts were reversed it would not be wrong to overcall with one spade.

(2) North is not contesting against his partner's spades, he is simply showing where his values lie.

West led a diamond, won by the ace. South hastily entered dummy with a heart to the king and discarded a club on the king of diamonds. Then he played a spade to West's ace. Having noted his partner's 8 of hearts on the first round, West led a second heart.

South could see what was going to happen: East threatened to win the next round of trumps and give his partner the lead with the ace of clubs, for a heart ruff. With an ingenious plan in mind, South won the second heart in dummy. The position was now:

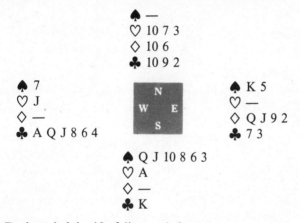

```
                    ♠ —
                    ♡ 10 7 3
                    ◇ 10 6
                    ♣ 10 9 2
    ♠ 7                              ♠ K 5
    ♡ J                              ♡ —
    ◇ —                              ◇ Q J 9 2
    ♣ A Q J 8 6 4                    ♣ 7 3
                    ♠ Q J 10 8 6 3
                    ♡ A
                    ◇ —
                    ♣ K
```

Declarer led the 10 of diamonds from dummy and discarded the king of clubs. His idea was to prevent East from giving his partner the lead for a heart ruff. But West played too well for him: reading the position exactly, West ruffed his partner's diamond trick and led the jack of hearts. East ruffed and the king of spades defeated the contract.

43. *Solo Performance*

Here is a small defensive problem. You are East and South, who has opened a weak notrump, plays in 3NT. West leads the jack of spades, implying a suit headed by Q J, and the dummy goes down.

<pre>
                    ♠ 7 6 2
                    ♡ A Q 5
                    ♢ 7 3 2
                    ♣ A Q J 10

                        N   ♠ 10 5 3
    ♠ J led   W   E   ♡ K J 9 3
                        S   ♢ A Q 8
                                          ♣ K 7 6
</pre>

Declarer lets the jack hold, playing the 8. Partner switches to the 8 of hearts—well done! Declarer plays low from dummy and you win with the jack.

The deal occurred in an Australian Championship. The Borins, Jim and Norma, the only husband-and-wife pair to have played in the final round of a world championship, were East and West respectively.

If you had been East and had won the second trick with the jack of hearts, do you think that you might possibly have returned partner's suit, leading the 10 of spades? It wouldn't have been quite good enough, for the full hand was:

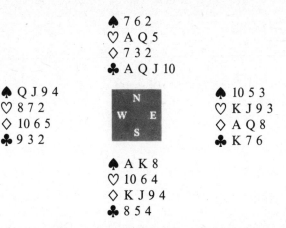

♠ 7 6 2
♥ A Q 5
♦ 7 3 2
♣ A Q J 10

♠ Q J 9 4
♥ 8 7 2
♦ 10 6 5
♣ 9 3 2

♠ 10 5 3
♥ K J 9 3
♦ A Q 8
♣ K 7 6

♠ A K 8
♥ 10 6 4
♦ K J 9 4
♣ 8 5 4

South was a point under strength for his opening 1NT, normally 12–14. However, he was non-vulnerable against vulnerable opponents.

West, you will recall, led the jack of spades and switched to a heart, which you have won with the jack. Say that you return the 10 of spades at this point. South will play a club to the 10, and whether you take this trick or hold up the king you won't beat the contract. South will play a diamond to the jack, then another club, which you win. There is no defence now to stop the declarer from making two spades, three clubs, and either two hearts and two diamonds or one heart and three diamonds, depending on how the rest of the defence is played. Your high cards will prove a continual embarrassment.

Jim Borin defeated the contract by means of a play that was both simple and clever: when in with the jack of hearts at trick two he returned a heart into dummy's A Q!

South did the best he could: a diamond to the jack, a club finesse, which lost to the king. East then played a third round of hearts and made two more tricks with the ace of diamonds and the thirteenth heart.

Remember this defence another time when you hold most of your side's high cards. Present the declarer with an extra trick early on in a suit where you can eventually establish an extra winner. If your play gives the declarer his ninth trick you will probably find that there was no defence anyway.

44. *Paper Darts*

Anyone who reads bridge books and articles knows about this kind of position:

A J x x

Q 10 x x   x x x

K x

Not needing three tricks from this suit, but needing two entries in dummy for other purposes, South leads low, intending to finesse the jack. West can frustrate this plan by cleverly going in with the queen. It is a play that everyone knows and almost everyone misses. But not on this deal from the Vanderbilt Cup, where Robinson and Boyd held the East–West cards:

Dealer East   Love all

```
                    ♠ 7
                    ♡ J 8 6
                    ◇ Q 10 8 6 5 3
                    ♣ 9 5 4
 ♠ K 5                              ♠ Q J 8 4 2
 ♡ 9 5 3              N             ♡ 2
 ◇ A J 4          W     E           ◇ K 7 2
 ♣ A Q 10 6 2        S              ♣ J 8 7 3
                    ♠ A 10 9 6 3
                    ♡ A K Q 10 7 4
                    ◇ 9
                    ♣ K
```

In these days weak two bids are thrown around like paper darts. After a pass by North, East opened two spades. South bid four hearts and all passed.

West led the king of spades and South won with the ace. Had there been no opposition bidding, South would probably have aimed to set up his spades (spade ruff, club to king and ace, trump, spade ruff, and so on). Knowing that the spades would be 5–2 or 6–1, South began instead by running a diamond to East's king. A club was led to the ace and West switched to a trump, won by dummy's 6. A diamond was ruffed by the queen and the position was now:

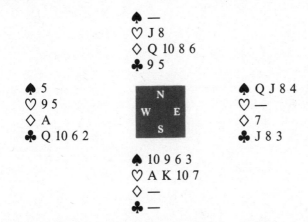

```
              ♠ —
              ♡ J 8
              ◇ Q 10 8 6
              ♣ 9 5
  ♠ 5                        ♠ Q J 8 4
  ♡ 9 5          N           ♡ —
  ◇ A        W     E         ◇ 7
  ♣ Q 10 6 2      S          ♣ J 8 3
              ♠ 10 9 6 3
              ♡ A K 10 7
              ◇ —
              ♣ —
```

South led the 7 of hearts and now, if West had played low, the declarer would have consulted his ancestors and probably reached the conclusion that the trumps were likely to be 3–1: he would have finessed the 8, ruffed a diamond high and made ten tricks. But Peter Boyd went in with 9 of hearts and South finished two down.

45. *Honours Even*

It doesn't happen all that often, but here is a hand from a North American championship where both sides played particularly well.

Dealer North   Game all

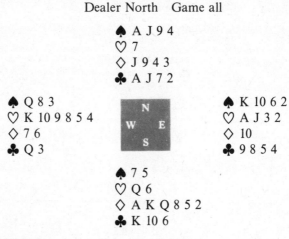

♠ A J 9 4
♡ 7
◇ J 9 4 3
♣ A J 7 2

♠ Q 8 3
♡ K 10 9 8 5 4
◇ 7 6
♣ Q 3

♠ K 10 6 2
♡ A J 3 2
◇ 10
♣ 9 8 5 4

♠ 7 5
♡ Q 6
◇ A K Q 8 5 2
♣ K 10 6

The bidding was well managed, too.

South	West	North	East
—	—	No	No
1◇	No	1♠	No
2◇	No	4◇	No
5◇	No	No	No

At the other table they finished in 3NT. Don't think it can't happen!

West led the 10 of hearts against five diamonds. When East came in with the ace of hearts he made the excellent return of a low spade.

After the ace of spades South negotiated a heart ruff and drew trumps. The position then was:

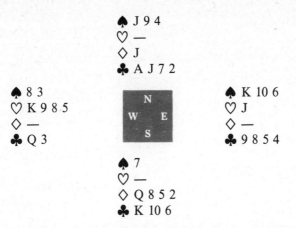

```
              ♠ J 9 4
              ♡ —
              ◇ J
              ♣ A J 7 2
♠ 8 3                          ♠ K 10 6
♡ K 9 8 5          N           ♡ J
◇ —            W       E       ◇ —
♣ Q 3                 S        ♣ 9 8 5 4
              ♠ 7
              ♡ —
              ◇ Q 8 5 2
              ♣ K 10 6
```

A club finesse now would have been dangerous. South found a better solution, leading a low spade to the 9 and 10. It seemed now that any play by East would give him the contract, but East smoothly returned a low spade.

Not sure about this, South ruffed and played off three more trumps, unblocking the jack of clubs to arrive at this ending:

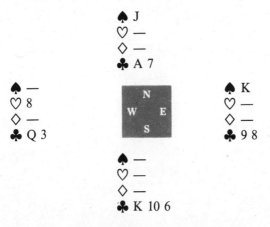

```
              ♠ J
              ♡ —
              ◇ —
              ♣ A 7
♠ —                            ♠ K
♡ 8                N           ♡ —
◇ —            W       E       ◇ —
♣ Q 3                 S        ♣ 9 8
              ♠ —
              ♡ —
              ◇ —
              ♣ K 10 6
```

After a club to the ace and a club back South had to do a little more thinking. Could West's last two cards be the king of spades and a heart? Not really; with K Q x x in spades and K 10 9 8 x x in hearts he would surely have overcalled on the first round. So South went up with the king to win a hard-fought battle.

46. *Crime Wave*

Sometimes, after an important match, a keen student of the game prepares a 'crime sheet', purporting to show who made mistakes and how much they cost. What a nonsense it is! A great deal goes on that is not recorded on the score-sheet. If screens are in use they make a little difference on some occasions—but only a little. Take a hand of this kind, which was played in the 1987 European Ladies Championship at Brighton:

Dealer West   Game all

```
               ♠ A 8
               ♡ 5 4
               ◇ A K J 9 6 5 2
               ♣ A 2
♠ Q 10 7 6 2                      ♠ 9 4 3
♡ Q 10 9 6 2                      ♡ A J 7
◇ 7                               ◇ Q 4 3
♣ 8 3                             ♣ K J 10 7
               ♠ K J 5
               ♡ K 8 3
               ◇ 10 8
               ♣ Q 9 6 5 4
```

The match was between Britain and Germany. When Britain held the North–South cards West led the 9 of hearts against 3NT, a lead that showed either two or no higher honours. In this case, obviously, it was two higher honours. She might have held K 10 9 x x, in which case it would cost a trick for East not to play the ace; but since East held a sure entry in dummy's long suit, this trick would scarcely matter. Working this out quickly, East put in the jack and South won with the king. This, as you can see, led to five tricks for the defence.

At the other table the German pair bid as follows:

South	West	North	East
—	No	2♣ (1)	No
3♣	No	3♦ (2)	No
3NT	No	No	No

(1) Artificial and forcing.
(2) Showing an Acol Two bid in diamonds.

Nicola Smith led ♡6 and Pat Davies made the same excellent play of inserting ♡J at trick one. Maybe she did this after a slight moment of calculation. At any rate, the German South paid her the compliment of placing her with A J x and ducked the trick. The defenders cleared the hearts, but East had no heart left when she gained the lead in diamonds. Ten tricks made and 12 IMP to Germany.

A big swing, and how would it have been assessed by a critic not sitting beside the table? Can you blame the British South or not? It all depends on whether East gave any indication of her dilemma. After all, it would look pretty silly to duck, then lose five tricks in hearts when West had led from such as A 10 9 x x.

And at the other table, where South held up the king, did East consider for a moment before playing the jack? The point we are making is simply that these things cannot be fairly judged away from the table.

47. *Diversionary Tactics*

It is surprising how many deceptive plays can be made with combinations such as Q 10, J 9, even 10 8. Whole chapters can be—have been—written about all of these. An example occurred during a women's championship in Cara Balleda, Venezuela.

Dealer South   Love all

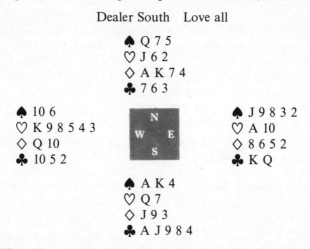

```
                    ♠ Q 7 5
                    ♡ J 6 2
                    ◇ A K 7 4
                    ♣ 7 6 3
  ♠ 10 6                             ♠ J 9 8 3 2
  ♡ K 9 8 5 4 3                      ♡ A 10
  ◇ Q 10                             ◇ 8 6 5 2
  ♣ 10 5 2                           ♣ K Q
                    ♠ A K 4
                    ♡ Q 7
                    ◇ J 9 3
                    ♣ A J 9 8 4
```

When Venezuela held the North–South cards in a match against Colombia, South became the declarer in the normal contract of 3NT. West led the 5 of hearts to her partner's ace, won the heart return with the king and cleared the suit.

At this point the declarer's best, almost only, hope seemed to be to develop four club tricks without letting West into the lead. Intending to play East for K Q x or K Q alone in clubs, she entered dummy by leading a low diamond to the king. West introduced a diversion by playing the queen of diamonds on this trick.

Now South, quite reasonably, formed a different plan. Hoping to make four tricks in diamonds, she abandoned the club suit and led a diamond from dummy towards the 9. West won with the 10 and cashed three more hearts to defeat the contract by two tricks.

Incidentally, what do you think of the declarer's play? I don't mean the miscalculation in diamonds, but the plan to play East for K Q or K Q x in clubs. Since she can afford to lose two club tricks so long as West can be kept out of the lead, the first play should be the *ace* of clubs. This would give her good chances if West held a singleton queen or king and would still be good enough when East held K Q alone or K Q x. And after the ace of clubs it would be better to cross to dummy with a spade than with a diamond, which might be a mistake if West held Q 10 x in that suit.

The club combination of x x x opposite A J 9 8 x also presents interesting possibilities. The point is clearest when the suit is divided 6–2, as here:

5 4

K Q   10 7 3

A J 9 8 6 2

Aiming to make five tricks, South begins with a low card from dummy and plays the 9 from hand, since his best initial chance is to find East with K 10 x or Q 10 x. West wins this trick with the king (or queen). Suppose that, on the next round, East plays low again. Then South will play the ace, since this will be his only chance to make the rest of the tricks without loss. To present the declarer with an alternative, East must play the 10 on the second round; then South will probably play him for Q 10 x.

Have you ever thought of this position:

K J 9 8 x x

A x x   Q 10

x x

South leads low to the 8. If East wins with the 10 South may do the right thing on the next round. But if East wins with the *queen*? Then surely South will play West for a possible A 10 x x.

48. *Two Nines*

Here are two hands with a similar theme—trump promotion. On the first deal East did not realize that his 9 of spades might be an important card.

Dealer South   Love all

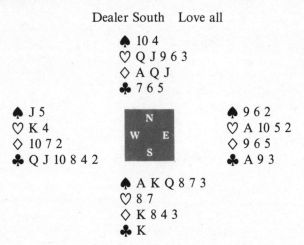

```
              ♠ 10 4
              ♡ Q J 9 6 3
              ◇ A Q J
              ♣ 7 6 5

♠ J 5                        ♠ 9 6 2
♡ K 4                        ♡ A 10 5 2
◇ 10 7 2                     ◇ 9 6 5
♣ Q J 10 8 4 2               ♣ A 9 3

              ♠ A K Q 8 7 3
              ♡ 8 7
              ◇ K 8 4 3
              ♣ K
```

North–South played in the obvious contract of four spades after this sequence:

South	West	North	East
1♠	2♣	2♡	3♣
3♠	No	4♠	No
No	No		

East won the first trick with the ace of clubs and, displaying a woeful lack of imagination, returned a club. Of course, it shouldn't have been difficult for him to judge that his side was not going to make any more tricks in clubs or diamonds. The only chance was to return a low heart. After two heart tricks East plays a third round, and then the defenders will surely win a trick in the trump suit.

When West complained of his partner's play, East said 'But South might have had a singleton king of hearts.' Unlikely, and it still wouldn't have been easy to construct a hand where the defence could take two trump tricks.

On the next occasion the mistake was made by the declarer, who gave the defenders an unnecessary chance.

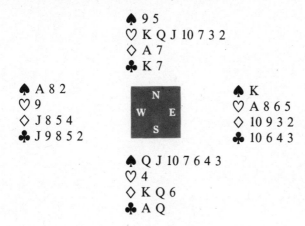

```
                    ♠ 9 5
                    ♡ K Q J 10 7 3 2
                    ◇ A 7
                    ♣ K 7
  ♠ A 8 2                        ♠ K
  ♡ 9                            ♡ A 8 6 5
  ◇ J 8 5 4                      ◇ 10 9 3 2
  ♣ J 9 8 5 2                    ♣ 10 6 4 3
                    ♠ Q J 10 7 6 4 3
                    ♡ 4
                    ◇ K Q 6
                    ♣ A Q
```

The best contract for North–South is 3NT, but in a pairs event the majority played in four spades after this bidding:

South	West	North	East
—	—	1♡	No
1♠	No	3♡	No
3♣	No	4♠	No
No	No		

Here South might have bid 3NT on the second round.

West leads his singleton heart against four spades and the defenders begin with ace and another. South ruffs high, but West is not so foolish as to overruff. Now at some tables the declarer led a spade to the 9 and king. East played another heart and this time it hurt.

These South players overlooked a cardinal rule—prefer to lead towards high cards. South should have crossed to dummy for the first spade lead. Then the defenders can do him no damage.

49. *Up to Strength*

Those of us who write textbooks are always happy when a textbook situation arises at the table and is expertly managed. Can it be, we wonder foolishly, can it be that our books are read in this or that part of the world? Such thoughts occurred when this deal from a ladies match between Austria and Poland was reported. The occasion was the European Championship at Brighton in 1987.

Dealer West Game all

```
                    ♠ J 9 3
                    ♡ K 5
                    ◇ A K J 10 7 5
                    ♣ A 10
♠ Q 10 4                                ♠ 6 5
♡ 10 4 2                                ♡ A 6
◇ Q 8                                   ◇ 9 4 3 2
♣ Q J 8 7 5                             ♣ 9 6 4 3 2
                    ♠ A K 8 7 2
                    ♡ Q J 9 8 7 3
                    ◇ 6
                    ♣ K
```

The bidding by the Austrian North–South pair may seem at first to be a little unbalanced.

South	West	North	East
—	No	1◇	No
1♠ (1)	No	3◇	No
3♡	No	3NT	No
4♡ (2)	No	5♣ (3)	No
6♡	No	No	No

(1) From the subsequent bidding it becomes clear that the Austrians followed the *canapé* principle; that is to say, the shorter suit was bid first on goodish hands.

(2) Was the South hand by this time known to be so strong?

(3) Apparently it was.

West led the queen of clubs, which had the effect of removing an important entry from the dummy. South won with the king and played a heart to the king and ace.

At this point the Polish defender, Mrs Zajackskowska, made an expert play: she returned a low diamond. (Who said 'Lead up to weakness'?)

The ace of diamonds won the trick and a spade was discarded on the ace of clubs. The position was then:

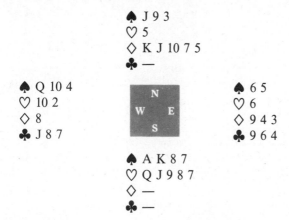

```
              ♠ J 9 3
              ♡ 5
              ◇ K J 10 7 5
              ♣ —

  ♠ Q 10 4                      ♠ 6 5
  ♡ 10 2            N           ♡ 6
  ◇ 8           W       E       ◇ 9 4 3
  ♣ J 8 7           S           ♣ 9 6 4

              ♠ A K 8 7
              ♡ Q J 9 8 7
              ◇ —
              ♣ —
```

One spade went away on the king of diamonds but it was end of the party for North–South when the next diamond was ruffed by West.

Well done by East, and an interesting thought occurs: what a brilliant play by the defender this would have been if all the time East (or West) had held Q x of spades, so that the discards were not needed.

[111]

50. *Tell Them Nothing*

Have you ever known the 2 of clubs to be worth its weight in proverbial gold? It happened at one table on this deal from a pairs tournament:

Dealer South   N–S vulnerable

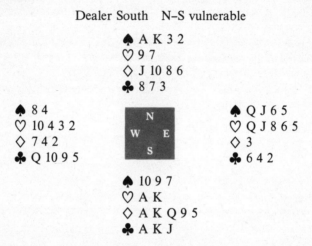

```
              ♠ A K 3 2
              ♡ 9 7
              ◇ J 10 8 6
              ♣ 8 7 3

♠ 8 4                              ♠ Q J 6 5
♡ 10 4 3 2                         ♡ Q J 8 6 5
◇ 7 4 2                            ◇ 3
♣ Q 10 9 5                         ♣ 6 4 2

              ♠ 10 9 7
              ♡ A K
              ◇ A K Q 9 5
              ♣ A K J
```

Some pairs attempted 6NT, a reasonable contract but likely to be defeated with the spades not breaking and the club queen on the wrong side. Others played in six diamonds after this type of sequence:

South	West	North	East
2♣	No	2♠	No
3◇	No	4◇	No
4♡	No	5◇	No
6◇	No	No	No

It is usually right to lead a trump after this sort of bidding where the declarer does not seem to have a strong side suit. However, at some tables West began with the 8 of spades. On one occasion South won in dummy and drew trumps, East discarding the 5 of hearts and the 2 of clubs—not a valuable asset, you may think. South cashed the top hearts, arriving at this position:

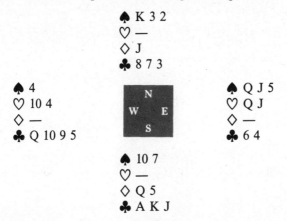

Assuming that West had led from a singleton or doubleton spade, it wasn't difficult to work out that East, who had parted cheerfully with a heart and a club, held at least three spades now and, probably, two hearts, as he would not have discarded a heart early on from four.

Backing his judgement, South played a spade to the king, cashed ace and king of clubs, then exited with the jack, leaving West on play.

Well done by South, but the most interesting point of the play was East's discard of the 2 of clubs. He wasn't going to win a trick with this card, true, but it is very important in defence to give declarer the least possible information. When South played a third round of diamonds it was certain that he had not begun with A K x x of hearts; on the third trump, therefore, East should have discarded another heart, not the club. Then South, quite possibly, would have taken the club finesse in preference to the other line of play.

51. *Look the Other Way*

The chess maestro, Bobby Fischer, once wrote: 'You have thought of a brilliant move. Bravo! But don't play too quickly. There may well be a better move.' East should have thought of that when the following hand was played:

Dealer South   Game all

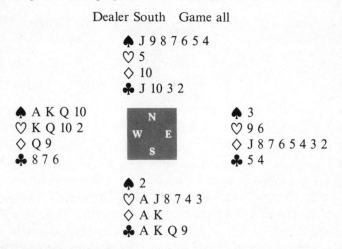

♠ J 9 8 7 6 5 4
♡ 5
◇ 10
♣ J 10 3 2

♠ A K Q 10
♡ K Q 10 2
◇ Q 9
♣ 8 7 6

♠ 3
♡ 9 6
◇ J 8 7 6 5 4 3 2
♣ 5 4

♠ 2
♡ A J 8 7 4 3
◇ A K
♣ A K Q 9

South opened with an Acol two hearts and West could only pass. The bidding continued:

South	West	North	East
2♡	No	2NT	No
3♣	No	4♣ (1)	No
4♡	No	5♣	No
No	No		

(1) Thinking it unlikely that the long spades would be of any interest to his partner; if North does bid three spades the final contract should be the same.

North–South had done well to finish in the most likely game contract. West led the ace of spades and on the second spade East discarded a heart. South ruffed, cashed ace of hearts, and ruffed a heart with the 10 of clubs. He returned to the ace of diamonds and ruffed a third heart with the jack of clubs. After a trump to the ace the position was:

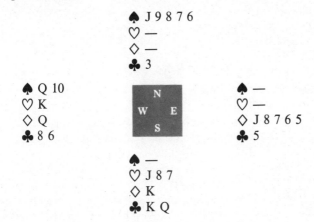

♠ J 9 8 7 6
♥ —
♦ —
♣ 3

♠ Q 10   ♠ —
♥ K   ♥ —
♦ Q   ♦ J 8 7 6 5
♣ 8 6   ♣ 5

♠ —
♥ J 8 7
♦ K
♣ K Q

South ruffed a heart with the 3 of clubs. East overruffed and . . .

This was a mistake, you see. South wins the diamond return and makes the rest. If East declines to overruff, then South must ruff a spade to regain the lead. He can make the king of clubs and the king of diamonds but he loses the last two tricks to West.

For East, it was just a matter of keeping up with the play. If he had thought about it he could easily have reconstituted the South hand.

52. *No Need to Cover*

Slowly, it is true, players have come to realize that the old injunction to cover an honour with an honour is often wrong. Most players do know about holding up the ace when sitting over dummy's (or declarer's) K Q 10. But have you considered the possibilities that arise from this position?

Q x x

10 x   A J x

K 9 x x x

South leads low to the queen. If partner has the 10 you can ensure two tricks by covering with the ace. But it's not necessary! If you would prefer to take two tricks in your own hand you can quite safely play low. South will let the jack hold on the next round, playing West for A x. The same sort of possibility arises when as East you hold A 10 x and West has J x: if it would suit the team for West to gain the lead you play low on the queen and low again on the next round.

Often you can spoil the declarer's entries with this kind of hold-up. At notrumps a suit is distributed like this:

K J 10 9 x

A x x x   Q x

x x

South leads low to the jack. If you cannot drive out dummy's main entry, let the jack win. South will repeat the finesse and may then be unable to develop any more tricks.

A clever play of this kind was made by Benito Garozzo in the 1963 Bermuda Bowl.

Dealer West   Game all

```
              ♠ 7 2
              ♡ 4 2
              ◇ Q 8
              ♣ K 10 9 8 6 4 2

♠ Q J 10 3                      ♠ 4
♡ Q 10 9 5      N               ♡ A 8 7 6 3
◇ 10 7        W   E             ◇ A 5 3 2
♣ Q J 5         S               ♣ A 7 3

              ♠ A K 9 8 6 5
              ♡ K J
              ◇ K J 9 6 4
              ♣ —
```

South played in four spades doubled after East had opened one
heart in third position and South had expressed his two-suiter. The
contract must go one down, obviously, the declarer losing two
spades and two aces. But somehow, with Benito in the East chair,
it went two down.

West led the 10 of hearts, won by the ace, and East returned a
trump to prevent diamond ruffs. South won, led a diamond to the
queen—and East ducked. A second diamond was led from the
table and again East played low. Naturally placing West with the
ace of diamonds, South let the 8 run. In with the 10 of diamonds,
West led a second round of trumps, and South still had to lose a
trick to the ace of diamonds. So he lost five tricks—two spades, a
heart and two diamonds.

Ducking the first—and second—diamond could hardly cost, if
you think about it. The ace was only going to win once.

53. *The Benefit System*

A great many contracts are made through a squeeze or an elimination play that could have been avoided by better defence. Indeed, it is quite rare for such end-play to be unavoidable. The declarer does not need to be an expert in this form of play: it simply happens that the defenders create their own misfortune.

Dealer South E–W vulnerable

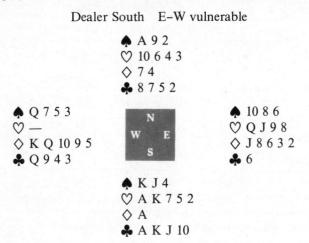

```
              ♠ A 9 2
              ♡ 10 6 4 3
              ◇ 7 4
              ♣ 8 7 5 2
♠ Q 7 5 3                      ♠ 10 8 6
♡ —               N            ♡ Q J 9 8
◇ K Q 10 9 5    W   E          ◇ J 8 6 3 2
♣ Q 9 4 3         S            ♣ 6
              ♠ K J 4
              ♡ A K 7 5 2
              ◇ A
              ♣ A K J 10
```

Wisely, as it turned out, North–South did not exaggerate their values during the bidding, which went as follows:

South	West	North	East
2♣	No	2◇	No
2♡	No	3♡	No
4♡ (1)	No	No	No

(1) South had a relatively weak two club opening and he was quite right at this point not to make any encouraging move. If South had bid four clubs, for example, North would have been fully entitled to show his ace of spades.

West led the king of diamonds and South's first thought was that this was the sort of hand where everything would be right and he would end with thirteen tricks. However, the first round of trumps dispelled that notion.

Not wanting to use the ace of spades too early, South tried the effect of playing off ace and king of clubs. East ruffed and returned a diamond, ruffed by declarer. South drew a second round of trumps and followed with the jack of clubs. West won with the queen and exited with a club to South's 10. The position was now:

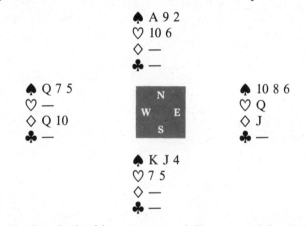

```
              ♠ A 9 2
              ♡ 10 6
              ◇ —
              ♣ —
♠ Q 7 5                        ♠ 10 8 6
♡ —          N                 ♡ Q
◇ Q 10    W     E              ◇ J
♣ —          S                 ♣ —
              ♠ K J 4
              ♡ 7 5
              ◇ —
              ♣ —
```

South exited with a trump and East was obliged either to concede a ruff-and-discard or open up the spades. Either way, the declarer was going to make his contract.

'Just as well we didn't go beyond the four level', South remarked, and the players moved on to the next hand. Nobody noticed that the defenders had made a small, but critical, error. When East held the lead after ruffing the second club he had no good reason to play a second round of diamonds: he could have exited with a trump, retaining the safe card of exit. Then, if South follows the same line as before, East ruffs the fourth club and leads a diamond, leaving South to tackle the spades without any help from his opponents.

54. *An Eye on the Entries*

The main lesson of this hand is that a defender who has long trumps (or whose partner has long trumps) should aim to weaken the declarer's trump holding even if this allows a ruff-and-discard. But it is also important to keep an eye on the entry situation.

Dealer North   Game all

♠ Q 4
♡ Q J 6
◇ A Q 10 7 5
♣ K Q 4

♠ A 10 8 7 6 5 2
♡ —
◇ J 9 6 3
♣ A 8

♠ K 3
♡ 9 8 7 5 3
◇ K 4 2
♣ 10 9 3

♠ J 9
♡ A K 10 4 2
◇ 8
♣ J 7 6 5 2

In a team game the bidding went:

South	West	North	East
—	—	1◇	No
1♡	2♠	3♡	No (1)
4♡	No	No	No

(1) East has enough for a raise to three spades at this point, but he may have thought that he should not risk encouraging his partner to save against four hearts.

West began with ace of spades and a spade to his partner's king. East returned the 9 of hearts and South's expectation of an easy game disappeared when the trumps were seen to be 5–0. Clearly he had to knock out the ace of clubs before drawing trumps. He led the king of clubs from dummy and West won with the ace.

Realizing that South had problems in the trump suit, West played well now by leading a third spade. The position at this point was:

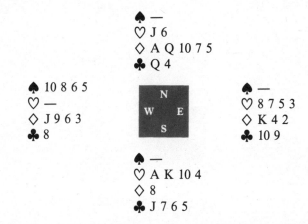

```
                    ♠ —
                    ♡ J 6
                    ◊ A Q 10 7 5
                    ♣ Q 4
     ♠ 10 8 6 5                          ♠ —
     ♡ —                                 ♡ 8 7 5 3
     ◊ J 9 6 3                           ◊ K 4 2
     ♣ 8                                 ♣ 10 9
                    ♠ —
                    ♡ A K 10 4
                    ◊ 8
                    ♣ J 7 6 5
```

South, who had lost three tricks already, had to ruff the spade with dummy's 6 of hearts. Now East did his bit for the defence by discarding a club in preference to overruffing. But South had the last word: he cashed the jack of hearts, crossed to hand with the jack of clubs, and drew the remaining trumps, discarding the queen of clubs from dummy meanwhile. Then he made the last two tricks with the 7 and 6 of clubs.

North congratulated his partner and West spoke for the defenders: 'At least we made it difficult for them', he said.

But not so difficult as it might have been. Not easy, but West must refuse to take the king of clubs with the ace on the first round of the suit. East discards a club on the third spade, as before, and South cannot come safely to hand.

55. *The China Syndrome*

An official team from the Republic of China, paying its first visit to a European event, played in the Multihouse Marathon Tournament in Rotterdam. The following deal is from an exhibition match which preceded the main tournament.

Dealer East   Love all

North
♠ A 10 8 3
♡ Q 6 5 3
♢ 4 3
♣ K Q 3

West
♠ J 9 7 6 5
♡ 10
♢ J 9 6 5
♣ 9 8 4

East
♠ Q 4
♡ A J 9 7 4 2
♢ 10 2
♣ J 6 2

South
♠ K 2
♡ K 8
♢ A K Q 8 7
♣ A 10 7 5

The Chinese East opened with a Multi two diamonds, signifying on most occasions a weak two bid in one of the majors. The bidding continued:

South	West	North	East
—	—	—	2♢
Dble (1)	No	No	2♡
3NT	No	4NT (2)	No
5♡	No	6NT	No
No	No		

(1) Apparently a penalty double, showing strength in diamonds. It is more usual to double with general strength.

(2) Blackwood, apparently. The alternative, when partner has bid notrumps and no suit has been agreed, is to use four clubs to ask for aces.

West led the 9 of clubs against 6NT. The declarer might have let this run to the 10, but it was very unlikely that West would have led from a long suit headed by the jack and South played well by taking the trick in dummy. He followed with a low heart from the table. East quite rightly ducked; if he goes up with the ace he presents the declarer with eleven top tricks, and a squeeze against West would surely follow.

South now cashed three more tricks in clubs and followed with three top diamonds and a fourth diamond which left West on play in this position:

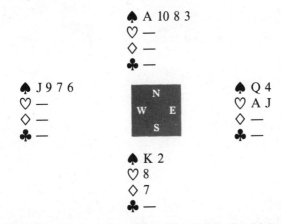

                    ♠ A 10 8 3
                    ♡ —
                    ◇ —
                    ♣ —

    ♠ J 9 7 6   ♠ Q 4
    ♡ —   N   ♡ A J
    ◇ —   W   E   ◇ —
    ♣ —   S   ♣ —

                    ♠ K 2
                    ♡ 8
                    ◇ 7
                    ♣ —

Forced to open up the spades, West led the 7, which was covered by dummy's 8. Now Wang Jungren, East, did not make the mistake of contributing the queen; he played low and South was unable to develop a twelfth trick.

56. *Money Men*

Representatives of many of the City of London's financial institutions took part in a tournament hosted by international chartered accountants, Price Waterhouse, in 1987. The event raised over £10,000 for The Prince's Trust. Distinguished visitors (in a bridge sense) were much interested in the following hand, which was dealt by East with North–South vulnerable:

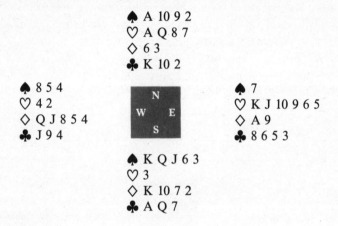

```
                    ♠ A 10 9 2
                    ♡ A Q 8 7
                    ◇ 6 3
                    ♣ K 10 2
    ♠ 8 5 4                              ♠ 7
    ♡ 4 2              N                 ♡ K J 10 9 6 5
    ◇ Q J 8 5 4    W       E             ◇ A 9
    ♣ J 9 4              S               ♣ 8 6 5 3
                    ♠ K Q J 6 3
                    ♡ 3
                    ◇ K 10 7 2
                    ♣ A Q 7
```

The slam on the North–South cards is borderline, but it was reached at some tables where the bidding was on three lines:

South	West	North	East
—	—	—	No (1)
1♠	No	4♣ (2)	No
4◇	No	4♡	No
4NT	No	5♡	No
6♠	No	No	No

(1) Weak two bids would not normally be played in an event of this kind.

(2) A conventional way of expressing a hand that is worth a raise to game and is not unsuitable for slam.

A diamond lead is dangerous and most West players began with a trump against six spades. An inexperienced declarer might draw three rounds of trumps before leading a diamond from dummy. This line fails, obviously, because only one trump is left for the two losing diamonds.

A good player would win the trump lead in dummy and lead a diamond from the table at once. There is nothing the defence can do then to prevent two diamond ruffs.

The interesting play occurs when declarer makes the slightly inaccurate play of drawing *two* rounds of trumps before leading a diamond from dummy. Still all right, you think, since East has no more trumps?

But East has had an opportunity to make his name by discarding the ace of diamonds on the second round of spades. After a diamond to the king the position is:

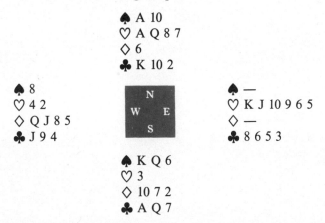

```
              ♠ A 10
              ♡ A Q 8 7
              ◇ 6
              ♣ K 10 2
  ♠ 8                        ♠ —
  ♡ 4 2           N          ♡ K J 10 9 6 5
  ◇ Q J 8 5    W     E       ◇ —
  ♣ J 9 4         S          ♣ 8 6 5 3
              ♠ K Q 6
              ♡ 3
              ◇ 10 7 2
              ♣ A Q 7
```

When West wins the next round of diamonds he leads his third trump and South is a trick short.